SECRETS OF SMALL GARDENS

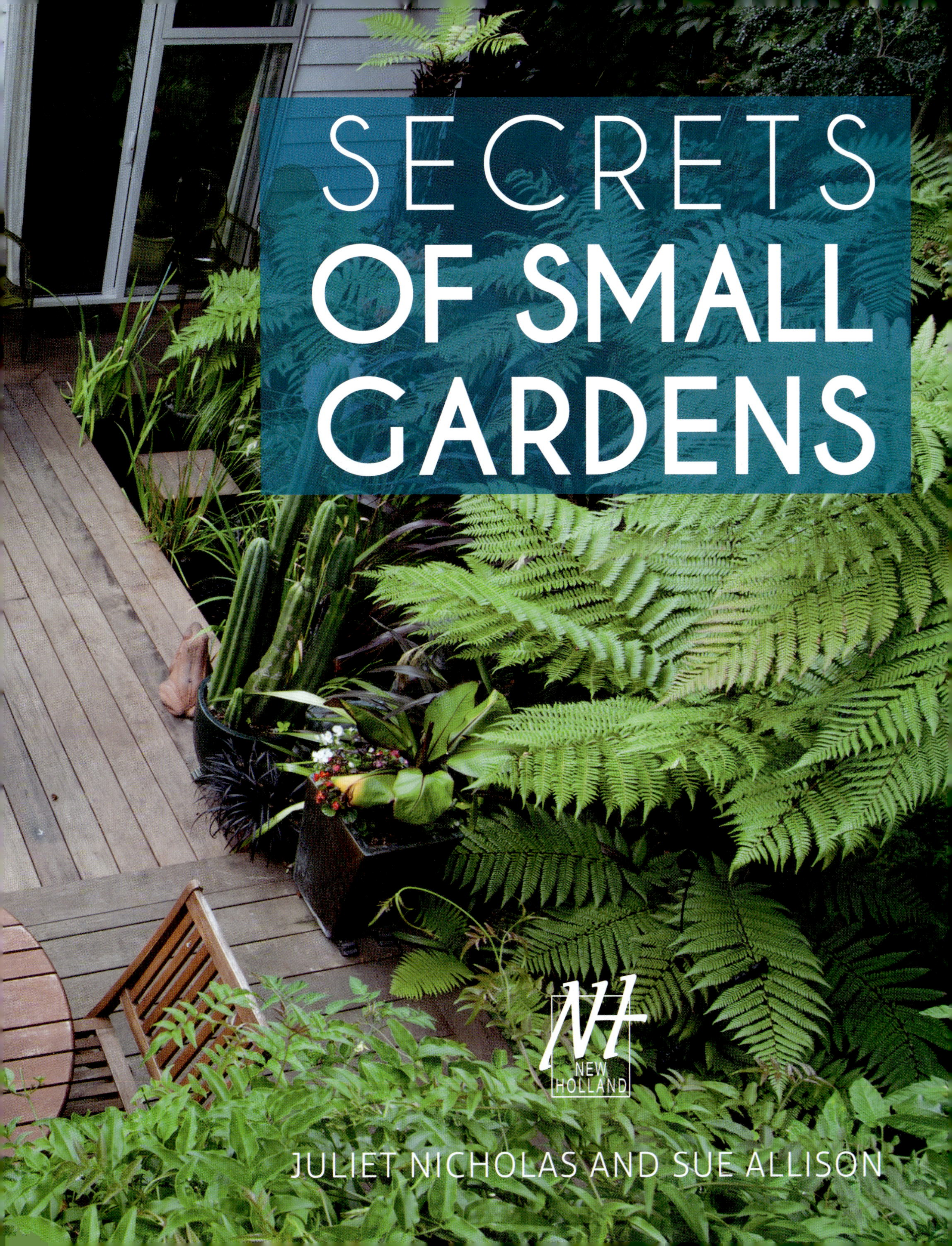

SECRETS OF SMALL GARDENS

NEW HOLLAND

JULIET NICHOLAS AND SUE ALLISON

CONTENTS

34

79

102

180

116

288

165

196

FOREWORD

Diminished dimensions certainly need not mean compromise. Small gardens can exude an intensity, intimacy and immediacy rarely found in their larger counterparts.

The small gardens featured in this book are all cleverly curated habitats, inspired rather than limited by their size.

At the heart of their success lies careful consideration as to how to best use the space available. "When you've got a big garden, you can have a bit going on here and a bit going on there. When you've got a small space, you have to make choices," says Jude Trengrove *(Escape to the City).* Or, as Juliet Mannering puts it: "I only have room for the things I love." *(The Front Room).*

Designing one's habitat is a highly personal affair and these gardens reflect a diversity of human preferences. "Less is more," asserts the creator of a minimalist sanctuary *(Rooftop Reverie).* "More is more," enthuses Warren Robertson of his bursting bijou backyard *(Inner-city Exotica).* Angie Gawith spurns "stressful colour" for restful green *(Downtown Seclusion),* while flowers are "food for the soul" for Jane Teasdale *(In the Pink).* Some pack their plots with edibles *(Framed with Fruit, Edible Artistry);* others favour naturalistic plantings *(Natural Connections).*

'Small' is a relative concept, linked to proposed use of space as much as meterage. A 30sqm courtyard is small by any definition, but so is a regular-sized backyard when it becomes the footprint for a subtropical jungle.

"Grow up," advises Mark van Kaathoven, dwarfed by towering palms in a garden three times as high as it is wide *(Growing Up).* Vertical structure and layering become all the more important when you are trying to make the most of every square meter, be it ground or air space.

Others use optical illusions to suggest greater space *(Garden of Illusion)* or defy their properties' perimeters by borrowing from the neighbors, be it the leafy backdrop of a park next door *(Parkside in the City)* or a cityscape viewed over the living wall of a seventh-storey balcony *(Room with a View).*

As people increasingly find themselves in smaller urban quarters or deliberately down-size, the garden becomes an even more important "room" in which to entertain, seek refuge or satisfy the senses.

Gardens, unlike interiors, are furnished with living things and their success depends on a sound knowledge of plants and how they will behave. When space is at a premium, the relationship between man and nature is more intense, the garden's secrets more intimate and the realisation of the creator's vision all the more inspiring.

Juliet Nicholas and Sue Allison

A cantilevered deck offers the ultimate in indoor-outdoor living on a lush sloping section.

CHAPTER 1

Subtropical Playground

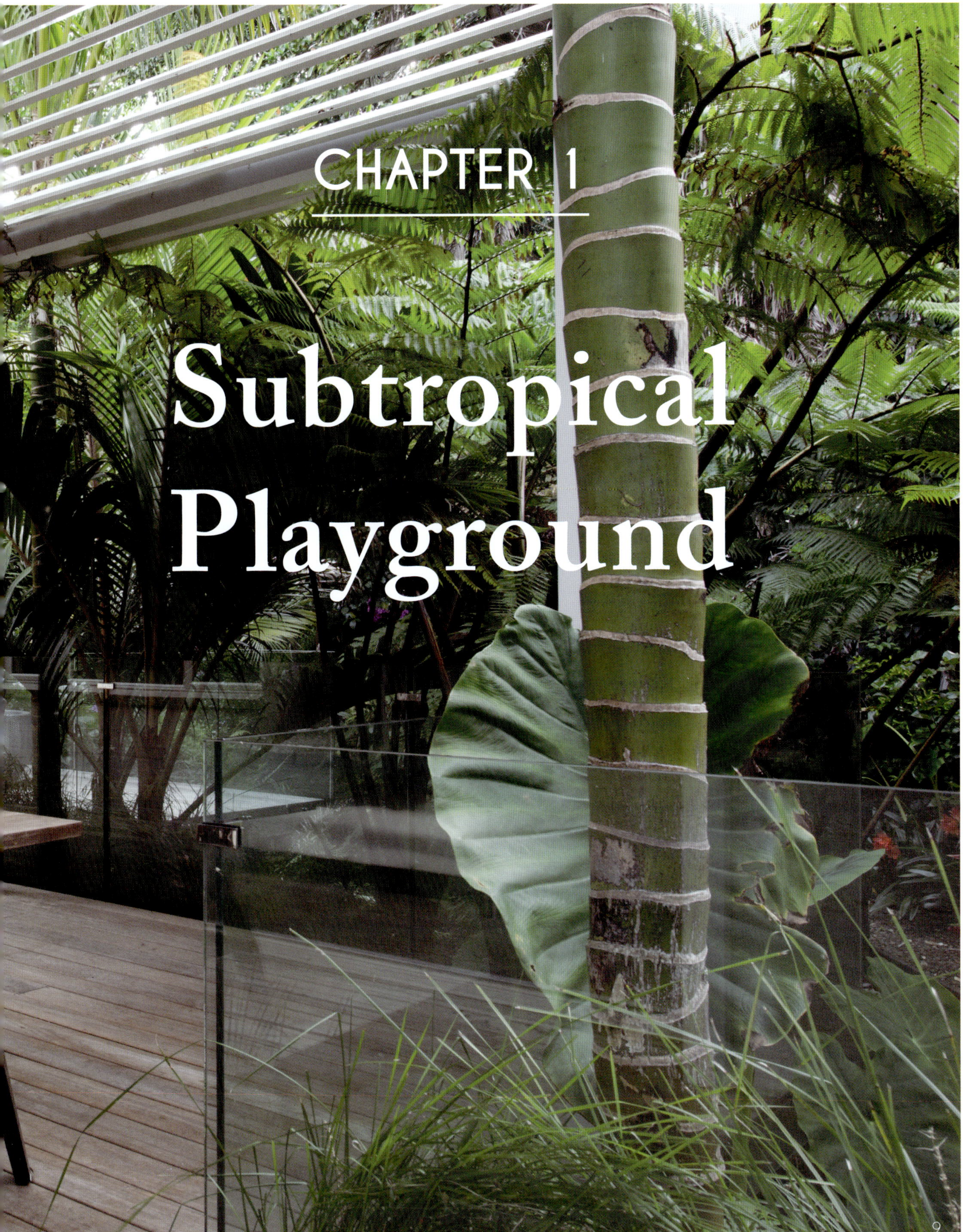

We wanted to feel as if we were in the middle of the bush, not in a city suburb.

A cantilevered deck, bridge over a small stream and luxuriant planting have turned a bushy suburban backyard into a subtropical playground.

When Tina and Tom Clyma and their two children moved to the property, the house opened to a dark-stained deck which was surrounded by a black corrugated iron fence and had little connection with the garden.

"We wanted to feel as if we were in the middle of the bush, not in the middle of a city suburb," says Tom.

By reconfiguring the deck and enhancing the natural features, they have created an outdoor living space that is fully immersed in its lush surroundings and connected with the small stream at the bottom of the property.

On Previous Page:
The outdoor fireplace and chimney gives the feel of a jungle megalith with tall plantings of Kermadec nikau and kentia palms, tree ferns and cabbage trees encroaching on the human habitat.

Neutral tones and monochromatic accessories add to the sense of tranquility in the garden. The vitex deck is screwed down rather than nailed for a sleek finish.

The new deck is cantilevered into the bush and built of vitex, a creamy-gray hardwood from the Solomon Islands. It has two distinct living spaces: an outdoor dining area under a louvered roof and a larger entertaining area with wood-burning fireplace as its focal point. In place of the previous visual barrier, a glass balustrade wraps around the deck opening both the house and outdoor seating areas to intimate leafy views and drawing the eye to the stream below.

The feet, too, are drawn to the water with a Monterey cypress jetty cum bridge leading from the deck and extending across the creek. On the other side, a stony path weaves along the bank and appears to head into the bush. While, in fact, it only goes a short distance, the effect is evocative, suggesting a path into a deeper jungle. The drama is increased at night with uplights illuminating the vegetation which, come dawn, resounds with birdsong.

A short flight of giant steps, fashioned out of concrete but resembling flat-topped rocks, leads down to the stream where the children spend many an hour playing in the water or feeding the eels. The over-sized rocks are matched by large-leafed plants and the four-meter fronds and fleshy monkey tails of Australian tree ferns.

With Tina's Tongan heritage and Fiji the family's favorite holiday destination, it's not surprising that the garden has a Pacific feel with its palms, bamboo and edible taro along the stream's bank.

"We wanted a lush and leafy environment with minimal maintenance," says Tom. "I never have to mow a lawn or trim a hedge. We just do a bit of weeding every few months."

That leaves plenty of time to relax and, not surprisingly, the family no longer feel the need to pack their bags and head to Fiji to do so.

Cluster palm (*Chamaedorea costarica*).

Top Left:
The outdoor fireplace and chimney gives the feel of a jungle megalith with tall plantings of Kermadec nikau and kentia palms, tree ferns and cabbage trees encroaching on the human habitat.

Bottom Left:
Comfortable contemporary woven furniture in steely gray sits lightly on the silvered vitex hardwood deck while a glass balustrade keeps the deck's connection with the garden alive and intimate.

Left:
An Australian tree fern *(Cyathea cooperi)* adds drama and structure with its huge fronds.

Right:
A recycled teak outdoor dining table gets year-round use under the louvered roof.

IDEAS:

Cantilevering a living space into a small garden maximizes the use of space, creates an intimate connection with the environment and gives lightness to a solid form. The ethereal effect is completed with a glass balustrade.

The deck steps down through a glass gate to a bridge over the stream. The stream, alive with eels and other wildlife, can become a torrent after heavy rains.

The wide bridge offers a chance to linger over the stream before descending to a gravel path on the far side.

Orange clivias make a flamboyant show on the path which appears to head into deeper bush.

Jetty-like posts anchor the bridge to the stream banks.

Kentia palm and fruit.

Orange clivias.

Vireya rhododendron.

Edible taro.

A cantilevered deck offers the ultimate in indoor-outdoor living on a lush sloping section.

Raised beds anchor a garden bursting with edibles.

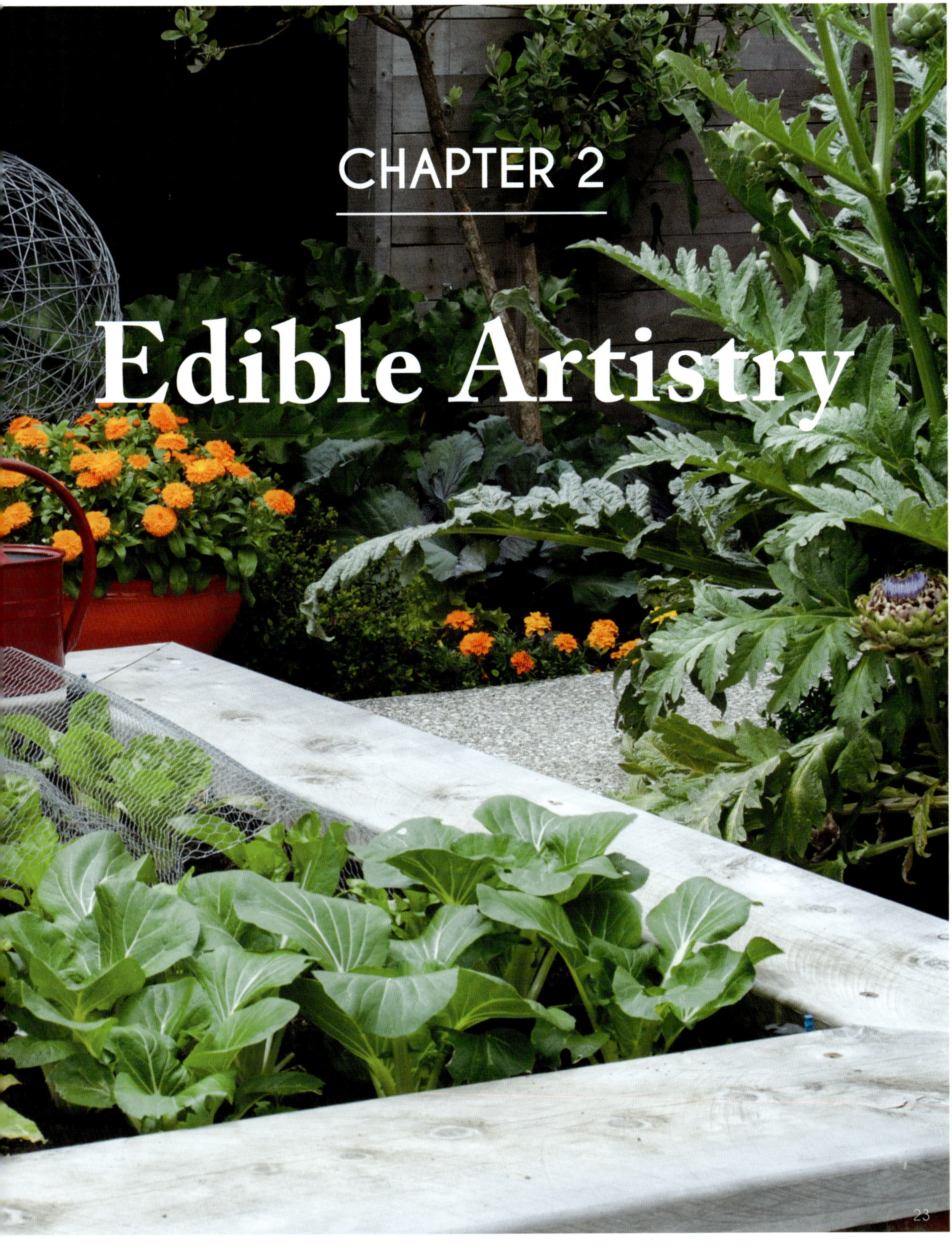

CHAPTER 2

Edible Artistry

Raised beds with wide Monterey cypress capping confine the edibles and provide seating in the garden while columnar dwarf *Ballerina Bolero* apple trees, climbing frames and a cherry-red obelisk give year-long vertical structure.

Our garden is visual, edible, inspirational and therapeutic.

If Monet found his inspiration in fields of flowers, Jenny Gillies — a fabric artist famed for her flamboyant floral creations — finds hers in her idyllic backyard.

Jenny and husband John have packed their small garden with edibles with a view to feeding not just the body, but also the mind and soul. "I see something in the garden, draw it, then develop patterns and create it," says Jenny, whose costumes portraying aspects of the plant kingdom have appeared on catwalks around the globe. "Our garden is visual, edible, inspirational and therapeutic."

Given the profusion of planting in the potager, hard landscaping is all the more important. The garden is anchored by three rectangular raised brick beds, capped with Monterey cypress planks that double as seating, and surrounded by aggregate paving and a small lawn. Concrete pots flank steps from the house, making an inviting entrance and adding to the symmetry.

Pyramidal dwarf fruit trees, wire balls and a cherry-red obelisk add height and drama in a garden in which all manner of edibles have been mixed to artistic effect. Orange marigolds sit amongst lush plantings of rhubarb, rosemary and citrus trees; standard bay trees happily share their bed with broad beans. A young fig tree grows alongside a feijoa with blue borage and the dainty white flowers of seeding coriander straying at its feet.

It is astonishing just what comes out of this 70 m^2 patch. The cornucopia of comestibles includes nine varieties of fruits: apple, nectarines, pears, apricots, prune plums, mandarins, limes, feijoas and a fig. Then there are the berries: raspberries, strawberries, cranberries, boysenberries, orange berries, blackcurrants, kiwiberries, grapes and gooseberries. Amongst them grow vegetables, herbs and edible blooms.

Even the fledgling camellia hedge is not a regular garden variety but *Camellia sinensis,* the tea-making kind. "We eat everything except the robinias and the box," says Jenny.

Squadrons of bumblebees, berry-thieving birds and small clouds of white butterflies share the spoils, uninvited but tolerated, while a farm of tiger worms recycles household waste in the far corner.

Edibles that escape the plate are encouraged to flower, seed and proliferate. Jenny calls it companion planting but the inhabitants of this small plot are far more intimate than that. They embrace, intertwine and sometimes smother each other and, come late summer, the overblown brassicas and dessicated pea pods become the inspiration for new designs for an artist who is more than happy to sew what she reaps.

Pak choy, beans and lettuces.

Beetroot, fledgling beans and lettuces.

A cherry-red obelisk adds height and drama to a raised bed with cabbages burgeoning at its feet. A bright potted marigold embellishes an arrangement of wire balls behind.

IDEAS:

Raised beds pay hefty dividends despite the set-up cost: they give structure and height, can double as seating areas, contain the spread of weeds and are easy on a gardener's back.

Below:
Silverbeet seedlings need protection from birds.

Night lighting transforms the seating area which features a wrought iron gate from the original garden as a decorative feature on the copper-capped Monterey cypress fence, and a grapevine trained over a sculptural wire goblet beyond the vintage French table.

An array of alliums and yellow-flowering arugula under a miniature apple tree screen a lounger on the tiny lawn. A row of standard bay trees line the side fence in the background.

The bold foliage of an artichoke softens the stepped entrance.

Above:
Elevated urns topped with buxus balls flank steps into the garden from the house, adding symmetry and a sense of order to the freely planted beds below.

Left:
Bee-friendly blue borage is profuse beyond the netted bamboo arches protecting strawberries.

Far Left:
A built-in seating area is tucked into the garden strip along the east side of house with a feijoa and fig tree providing a dappled screen and continuing the edible theme.

Marigolds make a bright splash among large brassicas.

Borage.

Spinach thrives in an old wine barrel.

Tomato seedlings.

Artichoke.

Broad beans.

Jenny uses cloches to nurture seedlings at the beginning of spring.

Strawberries.

Jenny's costumes portraying aspects of the plant kingdom have appeared on catwalks around the globe. Here, a model poses in the garden as a scarlet runner bean.

A balcony garden looks over a living wall to sweeping views of the city skyline.

CHAPTER 3

Room with a View

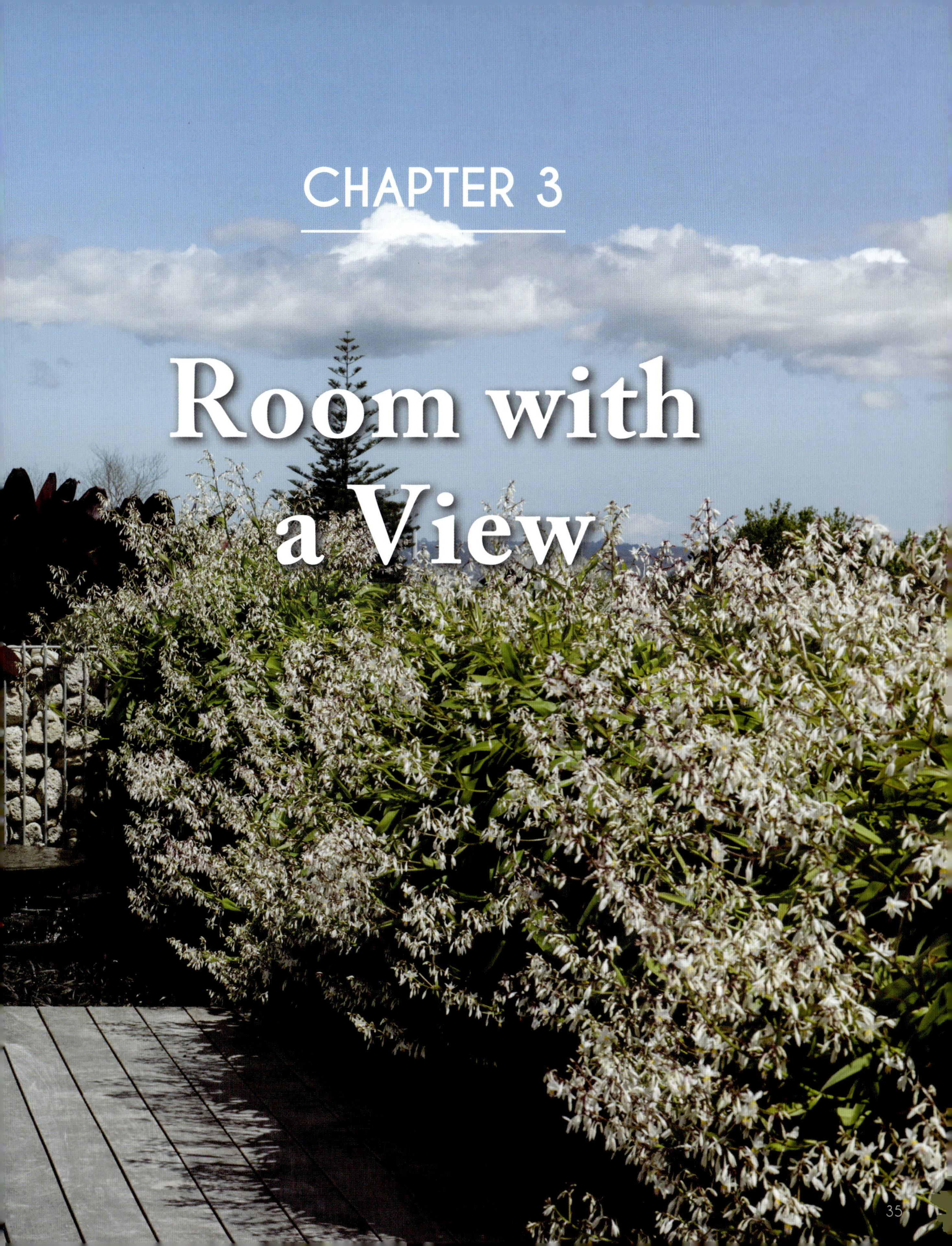

Breakfast alfresco is an elevated affair. The small table outside the kitchen-living area, which catches the morning sun as well as sky-high city views, is grounded by palms in planter boxes and a green trimmed wall.

A shallow water bath behind safety glass in the walled garden is an inviting stopover spot for high-flying birds as well as green relief amongst the cityscape.

I never realised the city was so green until we came up here.

Borrowing from your neighbors is always a good scheme when creating a garden in a confined space, and the inhabitants of this inner-city apartment have done just that on a grand scale.

Peter and Nicola Jeffares' seventh-floor balcony looks over a verdant balustrade to sweeping vistas of a cityscape dotted with parks and treetops and the harbor as its backdrop. The planting within the confines of their lofty garden gives them a sheltered and tranquil immediate environment; the living wall creates a green-fringed infinity edge that enhances rather than blocks the view. "I never realised the city was so green until we came up here," says Peter.

The meter-high vertical garden extending along the front of the 20 m long deck contains only four plants: rengarenga lilies, mondo grass, white rata and elephant ear taro. Like the other plants on the expansive eyrie, they are exposed to the sun, wind and salt-laden air and have been chosen for their toughness as well as their contrasting textures and lushness. Embedded in an inert planting media, which has water and air-holding capacity but contains no natural

Pumice, being light in both weight and colour, is an ideal filler for the gabion walls and blends with the naturally silvering vitex hardwood of the decking.

Cycad foliage.

Textured cycad detail.

IDEAS:

Wheeled planters give the opportunity to reposition garden beds at whim, and also make it easy to resurface or clean the deck or terrace underneath. The wheels can be locked to secure them in place.

The loggia, with a custom-made splashback above the cooking area, is a much-used outdoor.

Neither inside nor out, the cut-back loggia is made all the more sheltered with a rain-sensitive louvered roof extending over the central portion of the balcony.

nutrients, they are fed and watered automatically three times a day.

The balcony garden features beds behind gabion walls at each end of the vitex hardwood deck. To avoid weight being an issue with this rooftop garden, the wire cage is filled with pumice rather than stones and the garden behind half-filled with polystyrene under potting mix, mulch and bark. Emphasis is on plants that perform well in the conditions but don't grow too big, such as bromeliads, coprosma and small cycads.

For safety, the gabion wall has been constructed using only vertical metal struts so children can't climb it, while the living wall is topped with glass to the required 1.2 m security level.

A miniature version of the Los Angeles Grand Park fountain at one end adds grandeur on a small scale, as well as drowning out the sound of traffic from the streets below. Beyond the fountain, a private corner leading from the master bedroom is screened by wheeled copper planters showcasing the distinctive orange and blue plumage of bird of paradise flowers and delicate jointed rain lilies.

At the heart of the balcony is a north-facing loggia, set back from the deck and covered with a rain-sensitive louvered roof. With its gas fire, built-in barbecue, comfortable seating and large waterproof TV screen, the sheltered enclave is neither indoors nor outdoors, yet both. Like the rest of this elevated oasis, it has been designed to capture the best of both worlds.

The gas fire and water-proof TV make it a convivial spot to watch movies and rugby matches.

Burgundy bromeliads reflect the rusty hues of the wheeled planters while the sea of white rengarenga flowers blend with the pumice of the wall.

Steel, timber, pumice and flowing water combine with highly textural plants.

Bird of paradise (*Strelitzia reginae*) flowers, with their striking orange and blue plumage, grow above delicate jointed rain lilies in the planters.

The water feature brings the tranquility of splashing water by day and is beautiful when lit up from below with everchanging colors at night.

A sculptural metal necklace adorning the wall repeats the hues of the steel and bold bromeliads above.

Rengarenga lily *(Arthropodium cirratum)*

A miniature version of the Los Angeles Grand Park fountain, the water feature sits in a stony pool under a bank of rengarengas spilling from the living wall.

Bird of paradise

Just four plants grow in the living wall: rengarenga lilies, mondo grass, white rata *(Metrosideros perforata)* and elephant ear taro *(Colocasia)*.

Black mondo grass and black bark blend to create a textured bed around the fountain.

A corrugated iron sheep grazing on fake grass mixes art with whimsy.

Man and nature have combined forces to create a carefully considered habitat that compliments the house and provides its occupants with a leafy sanctuary in the city.

CHAPTER 4

Downtown Seclusion

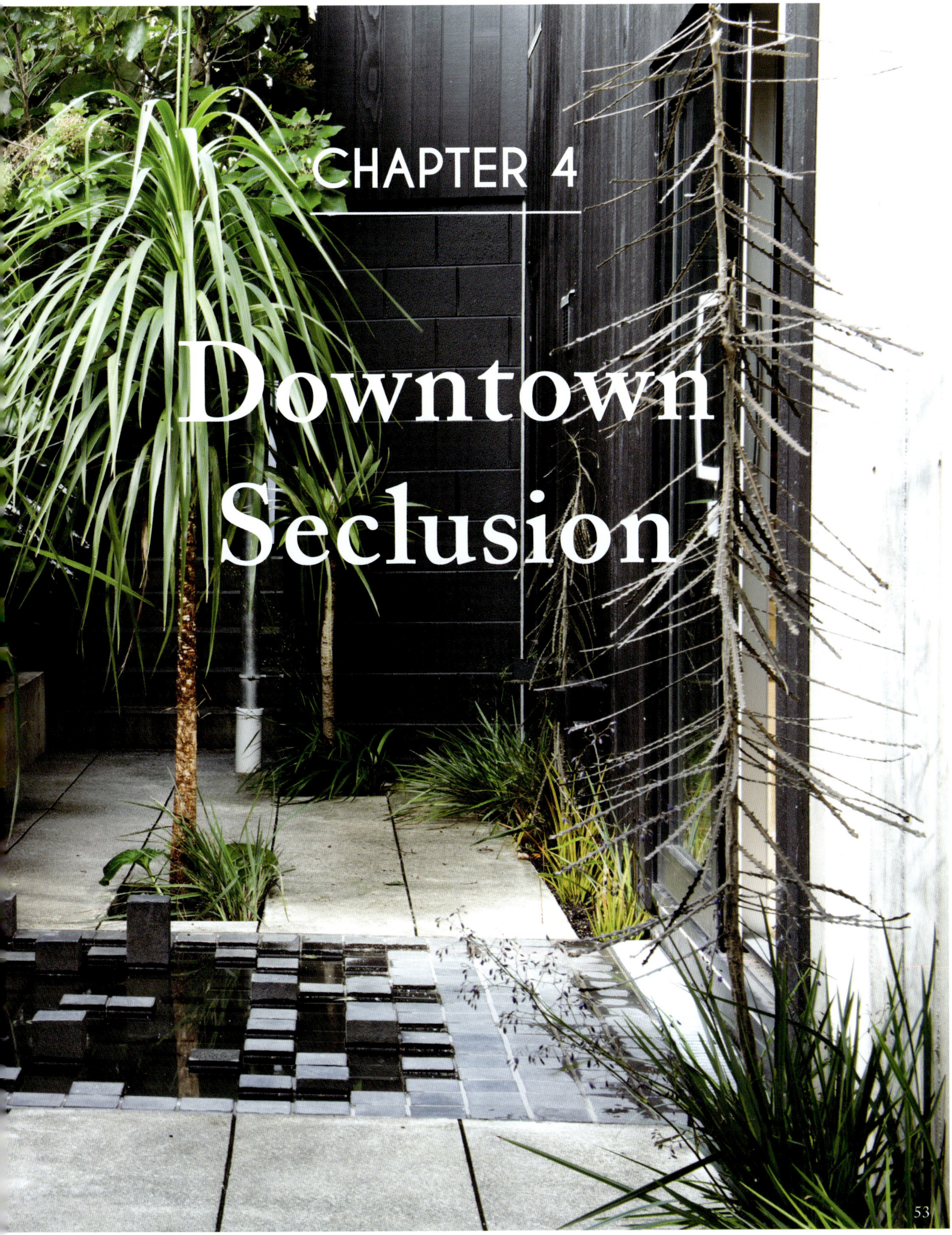

You wouldn't know you were close to the heart of the city.

Most people who want the convenience of inner-city living and a forest retreat have to buy two properties, but Angie and Richard Gawith have achieved both within one small section.

The 170 m^2 garden that wraps around their three-story house is never more than a few meters deep, yet through strategic planting and thoughtful use of materials, landscape architect Mark Newdick has created a habitat that is leafy without being gloomy, private without being sequestered. "You wouldn't know you were close to the heart of the city," says Angie.

Left:
The water feature is the visual and social focal point of the narrow garden with saw-cut Monterey cypress seats either side of a pond created out of staggered bluestone blocks.
A cabbage tree stands alone amid the paving with tall ribbonwoods, bushy Rangiora and a smaller mountain cabbage tree joining the silvery spears of astelia and wiry muehlenbeckia in the textured forest planting alongside.

It is a garden that both celebrates and softens the tall cuboid house, repeating its forms and honest raw materials while weaving them into a naturalistic setting. Squares are a recurring theme, from the garrison-like trellised steel gates at the entrance to the use of granite setts and concrete paving.

The back section itself is square, small and boxed in by its neighbors. "The immediate response is to plant high hedges which tend to reinforce the boundaries without giving any depth," says Mark. Instead, he stained the fences black, making them visually recede and suggestive of a shadowy forest beyond. To give privacy while retaining a sense of lightness, he strategically placed tall lean trees such as lancewoods and ribbonwoods above wiry shrubs, with rengarenga lilies and Chatham Island forget-me-nots adding lushness at ground level.

Staggered paving interspersed with areas of planted gravel adds to the illusion of expanse as well as blurring the hard lines. "I tried to create undulation around the boundaries in a structured way. I didn't want a swirly-whirly garden," says Mark, who also feathered out the driveway with an irregular edging of granite setts.

The ubiquitous square has its culmination in the garden's focal point: a sculptural fountain built of bluestone blocks set at staggered heights. A three-dimensional extension of the sett paving, it plays with the concept of water passing through landforms and, for Richard and Angie, has the added attraction of being a safe playground for their young grandchildren.

A similar abstraction of raw materials is seen in the seating area alongside, where hefty heart Monterey cypress benches sit on steel legs, giving them a sense of weightlessness that belies their bulk, especially when up-lit at night.

Muehlenbeckia and astelia add their own sculptural forms to the artistry created by the water feature tumbling like a rockfall between the saw-cut Monterey cypress bench seats.

Mark calls for calm and restraint when designing small gardens, with his favorite colour combination being "green on green on green with the odd bit of silver". Angie, who wanted neither flowers nor colour in her garden, sings from the same songsheet: "Colors can be stressful, especially if they are competing with each other. We wanted restful green surroundings and privacy, and that's exactly what we got."

Muehlenbeckia astonii

Lancewood
(Pseudopanax crassifolius)

Astelia

Far Left: The front door looks through an uncluttered glass vestibule to the garden's central water feature on the other side, which is a three-dimensional play on the square granite sett porch.

Center: A bird's-eye view shows the interplay of man-made design with that of nature in the narrow garden

IDEAS:

A successful marriage between house and garden begins by sharing materials. Hard landscaping that echoes the construction and form of the house will create an underlying harmony. Whether brick, timber, concrete or steel, raw materials can be repeated in seating, paving, walls or fences. Planting, too, can be used to carry the colour scheme from the house to the garden.

Left:
The heavy bench seat, crafted out of vertically stacked slabs of heart Monterey cypress, is carefully lined up with the cut-concrete paving and has an ethereal quality with its concealed steel supports.

The driveway melds into the garden with the raw materials of the house tying in with concrete paving and the black corrugated fence behind. Gravel was used in the parking area to reduce the amount of hard paving and create a courtyard feel.

The paved path to the spa is softened and made to feel wider with rengarenga lilies planted stepped into its irregular edge under bushy Griselinia 'Lucida'. Old brick of neighbor's house adds character to the corner spa area.

The sinewy stems of a Three Kings vine *(Tecomanthe speciosa)* weave through steel squares of a fence by the balcony steps.

The water feature adds another dimension to the square motif.

Strong steel trellising of the front gate gives the property a sense of security without being visually shut away.

Mass-planted rengarengas grow under cabbage trees and cherries along driveway.

Puka leaves add colour and contrasting round forms to the driveway edge, which is softened with feathered granite paving.

Asplenium oblongifolium

Ficus pumila

Cabbage tree leaves

In a play on classical symmetry, a suburban backyard has been transformed into a dramatic garden that looks to have been carved out of a jungle.

CHAPTER 5

Jungle Drama

It's a celebration of neo-Palladian symmetry with a Memphis-Gaudi-tropical twist.

The renovation of a classic villa in the 1990s set the scene for a dramatic garden makeover that saw a straggly backyard transformed into a dramatic jungle tableau.

From the street, passers-by still see a traditional white villa with a central front door. In homage to the classical symmetry, the entrance is flanked by a pair of ivy-clad orbs resembling monumental lollipop topiaries. But once through the portal, the descent down the villa's central staircase brings an ever-widening vista of a tropical stage set fringed with palm trees. Passage continues through two terraces to a dark reflection pool, behind which stand the pale columns of a Doric folly.

"It's a celebration of neo-Palladian symmetry with a Memphis-Gaudi-tropical twist," says the owner and co-creator.

The narrow sloping section, 28 m by 12.8 m wide, gave the owners the opportunity to create a terraced amphitheater with the house

The villa façade is a picture of conventional symmetry with only the oversized ivy-clad plaster balls a clue that there may be more to meet the eye.

n ever-widening view down the central staircase culminates in this ropical panorama seen through the wall-width glass doors opening rom the living area to the top terrace. The two very different plays n symmetry are linked by the subtle use of the same paving tiles at he villa entrance and on the terrace.

layout integral to the design. "Because the land drops away, the house looks over garden rather than into it." They made the most of this natural viewing platform by turning the lower floor into a full-width living space opening to the upper terrace through bi-folding glass doors. From the street to the folly, the house and garden are conceived as a series of rooms seamlessly stepping down via a medial pathway to the pool.

Neighboring houses share the elevated vantage point so privacy was part of the planting plan. A high wall of Bangalow palms forms a visual barrier as well as creating the illusion that the garden has been hacked out of a tropical forest that extends beyond. Exotic bromeliads, staghorn ferns and other epiphytes have been attached to the trunks, adding richness and depth to the backdrop. Below, colorful clivia, strelitzia and giant ligularias share the undergrowth with bamboo, cycads and fern fronds.

In another sleight of hand, the pool is not the regular rectangle it seems but a subtle trapezoid shape, its decreasing width giving the illusion of greater length. A bubbling water feature adds sound and movement to the performance while overhead an unexpected bough of cherry blossom extending from the jungle introduces a touch of whimsy. At night, lighting completes the carefully choreographed drama.

A gray-gold gravel path around the pool invites meditative circumambulation within the cloister-like colonnade of palm trunks. The palms, in their bid to catch the light, appear to lean towards the folly as if attentive members of an audience.

Anchored by strong hardscaping and large plants, this garden performs well with little prompting, leaving its inhabitants plenty of time to enjoy the show.

Left:
Tall Bangalow palms screen the Neighboring properties with a middle layer of banana and fan palms, cycads and bamboo dropping to an undergrowth of ferns, clivia, strelitzia and giant ligularia.

Right:
The mosaiced pillars and planter box with a potted yucca are a salute to Spanish architect Antoni Gaudi.

IDEAS:

Perspective illusions are based on the idea that objects appear to get smaller as we look into the distance. Renaissance painters in Europe were the first to play with the idea. Strong lines and a central path create the sense of elongated space, while a subtly tapering pool or avenue of trees of decreasing height can add to the illusion. Placing paving stones slightly closer together as they recede into the distance is another way of tricking the eye. All these devices depend on the garden being viewed from a central point.

The monumental kava bowl urns, which are the work of master plasterer Graham Mumford, are planted with *Bromeliad alcantarea imperialis* 'Rubra' growing over a bed of ivy. Their balled feet give them a sense of lightness.

Extensive paving, strong hardscaping and large plants anchor the garden and keep maintenance to a minimum.

Epiphytes growing on the palm trunks add to the textural layers of the subtropical forest.

The striking foliage of palm fronds and the head of the potted yucca.

Crown fern – *Blechnum discolour.*

Variegated green and white of a ginger plant.

Striking veins of *Calathea zebrina* with *Monstera deliciosa* in the background.

Light and water make a colorful play in the ivy-fringed reflection pool.

Doric columns with a jungle backdrop of glossy monstera pay homage to Western classicism and the concept of a folly.

Cycads grow under palm trunks which are hosts to epiphytes like this staghorn fern.

Far Left:
Monstera deliciosa **or 'Swiss Cheese plant' makes a dramatic foil for other foliage amongst the columns.**

The trapezoid pool tapers slightly giving the illusion of greater length and further drawing the eye to the columned folly at the end. Fringed with ivy (a low-maintenance groundcover) it is surrounded with a mix of lime-chip and river stones that tie in with the creamy paving used elsewhere.

An avenue of lime trees form a strong central axis as well as framing views through to both sides of a tranquil green garden.

CHAPTER 6

Green Retreat

The view west across the central pathway shows the subtle level changes and differing surface treatments that define the garden spaces, while the canopy of limes adds a green layer overhead.

A garden has more mystery if you can't see the whole thing at once.

An avenue of lime trees, garden rooms on multiple levels, views framed by tree trunks, a paved patio with a pond. Listing the elements of Ben McMaster's garden makes it sound expansive, but all this is within an 8 m by 8 m patch between the street and a small weatherboard house that doubles as the landscape architect's office.

When he bought the 1890 villa, the front garden comprised a clothesline in the middle of an overgrown lawn with a curved brick path to the front door. "A garden should be married to the house," says Ben, whose first act was to bring in a digger and raze everything bar a holly hedge at the front, reprieved for its ability to provide impenetrable privacy. He then carved the space into three distinct but subtle levels, the strips running perpendicular to the house and rising from east to west, each about 20 cm higher than its neighbor.

Ben laid a marble-chip pathway flanked by pleached limes along the central section, anchoring the garden with a strong backbone and defining the adjacent spaces without completely shutting them off. On one side, his office steps down to a sunken patio fringed with a low brick wall and incorporating a pond; on the other, his living room overlooks a restful garden in shades of green and white. From all aspects, the tree trunks frame glimpses through to both gardens. "A garden has more mystery if you can't see the whole thing at once," he says.

Overhead, the leafy lime tops have been squared off, creating high green panels in summer. "All the space above you is free. The pleached limes give me another living boundary above without encroaching on the space below."

IDEAS:

Different levels, however subtle, add another dimension to any garden, creating interest as well as defining spaces. Steps are always inviting, sunken gardens evocative and low walls not only act as physical and visual divisions but can be used to form raised beds.

A topiaried buxus in a terracotta pot stands as centerpiece in the square paved courtyard fringed with verdant green mondo grass *(Ophiopogon japonicas)* inside the gate. Beyond it, the path continues across the central pleached walkway to a sunken garden at the far end.

A classical urn and weathered seat sit comfortably with contemporary plinths and containers, the latter repeating the squares of the paving and all in harmony with the pared back palette.

The paved sunken patio, with a small pool behind the low brick wall at right, is a restful green space for sitting and entertaining.

The garden has been layered to make the most of the small footprint. At ground level, liriopes and mondo grass join ligularia and miniature irises, with silver teucrium and an array of hydrangeas rising to evergreen shrubs and small dogwoods. "It's all about texture and the juxtaposition of colour," says Ben, who also picks plants for their perfume, from michelia and white daphne to the jasmine draped along the verandah. "I love walking into a courtyard and being drenched in scent."

While there's a lot going on in this garden, it feels tranquil and uncluttered. "Don't fall into the trap of going to the garden center and buying one of this and one of that," he warns. "At least plant groups of three or five so you don't end up with a spotty garden."

By establishing a strong structure and sticking to a clean and simple planting palette, Ben has created the ideal home ground for someone who is busy and in the business: it both looks good and largely looks after itself.

Looking from the sunken courtyard through pleached limes and over mass groupings of mainly green plants which create a carpet that manages to be richly textured without being busy.

Left: Ben trained the branches of the limes along wires to encourage horizontal growth when they were young and flexible.

A buttery bloom of miniature iris 'Lemon Fizz' amongst ligularia leaves.

The limes are underplanted with the contrasting foliages of ligularia and miniature irises with a squared-off buxus bush adding formality by the front steps.

The lime-chip path leads from the holly hedge by the street to the front door, its crunch underfoot heralding the arrival of visitors.

An abstract limestone figure is a calm presence in the garden.

Ben's living room window looks over his "bowl of lilies" with the limestone figure visible in the background.

Droplets of water sit on the felted leaves of Lady's mantle (*Alchemilla mollis*).

Glossy leaves of 'Tractor Seat' ligularia (*Ligularia reniformis*).

Grey-green leathery foliage of the Marlborough rock daisy (*Pachystegia insignis*).

Heuchera, hostas and Solomon's Seal, chosen for their varying foliage and form, grow below an urn planted with a Marlborough rock daisy.

Variety is the spice of life in a garden where hardscaping anchors unbridled exuberance.

CHAPTER 7

Inner-City Exotica

I want natural overflow and a garden that's always changing.

Warren Robertson and Michael Corcoran's garden is reminiscent of a party to which a myriad of disparate guests have been invited and, to everyone's delight, all get along famously.

Their little leafy haven in an urban enclave defies conventions and that's the way they like it. "It's Bali hits the Antipodes, with a bit of Victoriana thrown in," says Warren.

Buddhas meditate amongst banana palms and bougainvillea; a coy cupid peeps out from behind ferns and fuchsias; ligularia and lilies share their beds with pansies and impatiens. A solitary 'Fairy' rose ("because everyone needs a fairy at the bottom of their garden") cohabits with a cactus. Even the stately copper beech that overlooks the back garden has let its hair down with scarlet tresses of Virginia creeper hanging from its boughs in autumn.

When the couple bought the property in 1996, the garden was plain and neglected. They started by ripping up large tracts of asphalt before laying a paved patio with walled gardens

A mannequin peers from behind a gate through vibrant purple bougainvillea.

Tree ferns and black phormium make a dramatic combination.

IDEAS:

Large-leafed plants bring drama and a touch of tropicana to a garden. The lush foliage of ornamental taro, an aroid belonging to the Arum lily family, exudes a jungle aura as well as creating a bold focal point that gives a sense of scale to smaller spaces.

off the living area and building a deck around the back, centered on a fishpond.

After trucking in soil and enriching it with compost, they set about establishing a luxuriant and lawless 'secret garden'. "There should be no rules when it comes to planting," declares chief gardener Warren, whose mantra is 'more is more'. "I don't like things to be formal. I want natural overflow and a garden that's always changing."

No inch is unplanted, including the narrow strip along the side of the house where runner beans share the fence with espaliered camellias and thornless blackberries, perfectly positioned to be viewed from a picture window in the bathroom. "There isn't much room for weeds," says Warren. Apart from an autumn clean up, maintenance is minimal.

The garden has thrived despite a major setback when their century-old Arts and Crafts brick house was destined for demolition after being irreparably damaged. Determined to save his precious garden, Warren dug up all the plants and put them in containers on the deck. For two years, despite living off-site, he watered and tended them and was rewarded with 80 per cent survival when they were replanted after a new house had been built on the original footprint.

The salvaged plants include more than 15 varieties of lush and exotic ferns, many of which normally do not survive in these chilly climes. Birds abound in the lush sanctuary and even some unusual stick insects have found their way to the garden. It seems no-one wants to leave this party and new guests, whatever their persuasion, will always be welcome.

Left:
Bird's eye view of the back courtyard's lush planting, surrounding the hardwood decking. A spa is completely hidden by dense foliage on the left.

The living room opens to a vibrant and leafy north-facing courtyard where a potted 'Flamboyant' begonia on the table repeats the hues of the cherry-red cushions.

Large leaves of a fan palm, ferns and taro create distinct layers that give a sense of order and stillness amidst the surrounding vibrancy.

Far Left and Middle:
The courtyard is a profusion of colour and texture with wheki tree ferns (left rear), *Phormium* 'Maori maiden' (right), variegated yucca, petunias, begonias and black mondo in the mix.

Below
Colorful pots and planting frame hidden treasures in the garden.

Striking red stalks of the *Ensete musa* banana leaves.

Contrasting foliage of taro and maidenhair fern.

Purple bougainvillea.

Buddha mediates beneath tree ferns at the end of the pond.

Simple planting and eye-catching hardscaping make a bold statement on an inner-city roof.

CHAPTER 8

Rooftop Reverie

Three plants of differing form and foliage are planted in staggered gray steel planters. The spears of Poor Knights lily *(Xeronema callistemon)*, leathery leaves of *Griselinia* 'Lucida' and mound of *Scleranthus biflorus* are made all the more dramatic by their graphic green backdrop in Resene Pacifika.

There's a reduced language up here.

A minimalist garden nestled amongst the rooftops of a bustling downtown area offers its occupants a serene sanctum above the city.

The 5 m by 7 m garden room sits above the couple's fourth story apartment in what was an old storage warehouse. A staircase leads from their open-plan living room to the rooftop which is alongside rather than directly above the dwelling, allowing a high window to look up into greenery. "It's grounding having a view of the garden when you are so high," says the owner.

With space at a premium, the garden's elements have been distilled down to a few shapes and colors. "There's a reduced language up here," she says of the thoughtfully edited area. The most graphic statement is made by a green gable wall, the surviving façade of a former building, now a vibrant backdrop for plants and eye-catching landmark in a monotone roofscape. Alongside, a gate-like steel balustrade repeats the angled profile, enclosing the rooftop room without boxing it in.

The floor is tiled with thick pavers propped up on jacks, keeping them clear of the sealed butanol underskin. Steel planter boxes of staggered heights but the same footprint have been slotted in to form the garden, allowing the layout to be changed at whim.

There are just three plants in the main group of boxes: *Griselinia lucida, Scleranthus biflorus* and Poor Knights lily *Xeronema callistemon*. Their contrasting forms and foliage combine to make a simple but bold statement with the lily's clumped spears, glossy ovoid leaves of griselinia and mossy mounds of scleranthus.

They have been selected for their performance, too, as the inhabitants of this lofty sun-trap have to be strong, easy-care and drought-tolerant. A pot is generous for *Griselinia Lucida* which can grow as an epiphyte with barely any soil; the Poor Knights lily, whose red flowers make a striking display in spring, does not mind being root-bound and will flower more prolifically if it is; and scleranthus likes nothing better than sun on its back.

Opposite, six vegetable planters keep the couple in leafy greens and herbs nearly year-round, as well as providing inner-city respite for foraging bees and butterflies.

The leathery ovoid leaves of *Griselinia* 'Lucida'.

The Poor Knights lily (*Xeronema callistemon*) has striking red flowers on tall stems in spring.

IDEAS:

Fashion designer Coco Chanel famously said: "Before you leave the house, look in the mirror and take at least one thing off." Editing is equally important in a small garden where well-considered choices and a minimal mantra can make the difference between a successful space or cluttered corner.

A cushion of *Scleranthus biflorus* spills out of its planter below its garden companions, a Poor Knights lily and *Griselinia lucida*. The trio is kept healthy with an occasional feed of sheep pellets and a watering system that is concealed under the pavers.

ANNAH'S FOOTWEAR FACTORY

The aromas of the city, including a nearby chocolate factory, and hum of air-conditioning units in a neighboring apartment block add an urban edge to the sensory experience. "There's a lot happening around us, but the surrounding buildings buffer the sound. It's peaceful up here," says the owner, who meditates daily in the garden.

At other times, the simply furnished Zen bolt-hole serves as a tea room, dinner destination or enclave for entertaining.

Like a green version of Coco Chanel's little black dress, the diminutive garden is chic and timeless, able to be dressed up or dressed down whatever the occasion.

A bench seat, carefully crafted with a back support, anchors the high fence on the street edge. The iron balustrade at the end, angled to mimic the surrounding roof pitches, encloses the rooftop room without boxing it in.

Right:
An evergreen rosemary bush grows behind seasonal salad vegetables in a garden that can be extended by replacing tiles with planter boxes.

Below:
Four planters grow prolific herbs and vegetables in the sunny sheltered spot. The pitched frame behind is a high window in the open-plan apartment below, with the stairway to the apartment through the glass doors on the right.

Herbs and vegetable seedlings.

An open backyard has been transformed into a private, shady courtyard roofed in Boston ivy.

CHAPTER 9

A Secret Garden

I can be indoors and still feel I'm in the garden.

Anne Bassett's tranquil courtyard is proof that dark clouds can indeed have silver linings.

When a two-story rest home was built close to her fence, it seemed her little backyard was going to lose all its privacy. Yet that space, which once featured a small lawn and rotary clothesline, is now a leafy courtyard, more secluded than before.

"You wouldn't know there was a building on the fenceline," says Anne, whose shady sanctum was created with a mix of hard landscaping and layered greenery. Three plastered concrete block columns were positioned along the boundary, with nautical wires running from their tops across to pillars alongside the house wall. Anne trained boston ivy up the pillars and along the wires, creating a green canopy that blocked out the neighbouring building and turned the space into a garden room.

Raised garden walls capped with terracotta pavers double as seating, while a row of olive trees and cedar shutters against the wall give the feel of a cool Mediterranean courtyard.

The front door is flanked by clipped teucrium in terracotta square pots with a lemon tree and white rose 'Gruss an Aachen' alongside. Pillars of ivy frame the entrance to the shady back courtyard beyond the front door.

IDEAS:

Gates to nowhere are evocative additions to small gardens where physical constraints prevent further perambulation. The door is a powerful symbol and even pointless portals fire up the imagination and suggest magical worlds beyond, along the lines of Alice in Wonderland's looking glass and C.S Lewis's wardrobe into Narnia.

Elsewhere the planting focuses on green shade-loving varieties selected for their form and texture. At one end, a mirror both disguises the garage and adds to the depth of the greenery while, at the other, a large window frames the view from the dining room.

In Anne's front garden, a pergola mirrors that of the courtyard garden but with wisteria clambering over solid beams rather than ivy on wires. In contrast, this compact garden is lush and layered, with a range of flora from roses to sub-tropical specimens densely planted around a small lawn.

For a plantswoman whose love of gardening doesn't extend to weeding, the solution was simple: cram things in so there's no room for weeds. There are more than 150 plant varieties in the garden, from sculptural plume poppies, Himalayan lilies and oak-leafed hydrangeas to muehlenbeckia, black mondo and lime-green euphorbia. Small treasures are poked in between or planted in pots.

"Apart from the roses, I'm not so keen on colour. I prefer green because it is restful," says Anne, who set out to create a "secret garden" full of charm and arousing curiosity. Stone frogs sit amidst ferns beside a mossy goldfish pond; a wrought iron gate set a meter out from the wall leads nowhere but suggests infinite possibilities; a short path through spires of buxus lures the inquisitive to a tiny corner dell.

The garden is designed to be equally enchanting from within the house, with every room looking onto it through large picture windows. "I can be indoors and still feel I'm in the garden," says Anne. "I've had numerous gardens over the years. This is my smallest but it's also my favorite."

A floor-to-ceiling shuttered window in the dining room brings the full effect of the garden indoors.

A shuttered mirror not only transforms the garage wall but reflects the greenery of the courtyard.

A trickling water feature placed by the mirror doubles the effect of the silvery surfaces.

A second shuttered mirror on the front wall gives the illusion of depth in a tiny space. When open, it reflects the layered greenery of maples, *Robinia* 'Lace Lady', Solomon's Seal, hostas and liropes.

Below:
A gray-green portal from the driveway is framed with the foliage of succulents, olives and Boston ivy.

No inch of the small property is unused. Vegetables and herbs grow in mussel buoys on the driveway.

'Windrush'.

A pair of white roses, climbing 'Iceberg' and 'Madame Alfred Carriere', drape the archway leading to the front garden.

Boston ivy.

Echeveria 'Crinkle'.

'Just Joey'.

'Gruss an Aachen'.

Giant taro leaves, ferns and purple ligularia are in the mix.

The foliage of ferns, ligularia, 'Green Goddess' lilies and *Monstera deliciosa* create a rich tapestry of texture.

Layers and levels, texture and topiaries are just a few of the elements in a garden that belies its size by heading for the sky.

CHAPTER 10

Growing up

The path leading up into the forested garden is half-hidden by a lush subtropical array of plants anchored by the sturdy trunk of the Dragon tree *(Dracaena draco).*

A figure in limestone reflects amidst greenery, pink spears of Aechmea and sprays of begonia.

You plant a garden and gradually Mother Nature moves in.

Mark van Kaathoven has defied the concrete jungle on his doorstep by creating a dense if diminutive subtropical one in his own backyard.

Mark's advice to plant-lovers with small patches is to grow up. "I'm using the airspace and the council can't charge me for it," he says. His verdant vertical plantation started with queen and king palms, Australian Bangalow and kentia palms but soon grew to include a diverse multitude that incorporated such varieties as the Madagascan Dypsis, shade-loving Lady palm and cold-tolerant Tibetan Sugar palm.

As his palms got taller, they become vehicles for more plants. A quarter of a century on and the towering first inhabitants are host to an array of aerial epiphytes that include brilliant bromeliads, delicate orchids, drifts of hanging Spanish moss and the beguiling green antlers of staghorn ferns. "It's like looking up at a stained glass window," says Mark, whose No.1 gardening aid is an 8 meter fireman's ladder bought in Kentucky by his American partner, Gene Dillman.

Below, tropical vrieseas rub shoulders with flowering cherries, lush greens mix with maples, and begonias bloom amongst succulents. Large-leafed ligularia and aspidistra inhabit the darker areas while clipped buxus balls and topiaries are evidence of human hands at work.

"You can have a lot going on in a small garden," observes Mark. The property is far removed from the house he bought in 1994, when its 270 m^2 garden comprised a sloping lawn, low wall of railway sleepers and swathes of oxalis. The son of a Dutch landscape gardener, who learned at a young age how to wield a spade, started by terracing the section with stone walls before creating three distinct garden rooms linked by bricked paths and steps.

He added water features, sculptures (Michelangelo's David poses on a carpet of mondo grass in an upper room) and whimsical touches (a "Dr Seussed" cypress clipped into cloud formations by the front steps) as, all the while, the garden kept growing around them. Originally designed to flow sympathetically from the house, it now envelops it. There is even a bromeliad plantation on the roof.

"You plant a garden and gradually Mother Nature moves in. The secret is to work with her and not try to control her," advises Mark, who leaves prunings and pulled weeds in the garden to compost as biomass, with birds scratching in the undergrowth aiding the process. Lizards scurry up palm trunks and the chirrups of small green frogs harmonize with birdsong in a backyard that is less a garden than a glorious man-made ecosystem.

The garden rooms are linked by bricked paths and steps.

Yellow and orange clivia line a pathway with clouds of tillandsia hanging overhead.

IDEAS:

Even the smallest abode will have room for Spanish moss *(Tillandsia usneoides)*. Neither Spanish nor a moss, these epiphytic bromeliads from Central and South America are known as airplants because they take in nutrients and moisture from the air through permeable scales along their leaves. They can be tucked into tree forks, draped over balustrades or hung from wire frames.

Brick pavers set in a patch of cream gravel add interest along the route to the large terracotta urn.

A vibrant orange clivia adds a flash of colour to the variegated foliage of a ginger plant.

David stands in a secluded dell bordered by clivias and spotted ligularia (*Ligularia tussilaginea* 'Aureomaculata').

Mark pollinates the clivias by hand.

Spotted ligularia (*Ligularia tussilaginea* 'Aureomaculata').

A selection of bromeliad 'Rubra' hybrids grow on the rooftop, adding their colors to the textured canopy.

Seeding nikau flowers.

Spanish moss *(Tillandsia usneoides)*.

Epiphytes attached to the trunk of a gray-green *Agave attenuata*.

Orange clivia brighten the forested path down the side of the house which is lined with shade-loving tree ferns and palms.

The pale pink cherry blossom is unexpected company for a cacti and subtropical flora, but it sits comfortably with the white colonial steps and its tresses are echoed in the cypress, clipped to a cloud formation, alongside.

Mark and Gene's verandah looks over plants from every corner of the globe with a myriad of forms and colors to match. Amongst them are cabbage trees, camellias, cycads and a cypress decorated with bromeliads and orchids.

Vriesea hybrids make a striking display in red and green.

94

Verdant Verge

Mark's zeal for greening the city and healing the ozone layer knows no bounds. In 1996, he started planting the roadside verge and it now resembles a rainforest, a profusion of birds frequenting the food-rich urban enclave.

"Why mow when you can grow?" asks Mark, who is passionate about the importance of creating green corridors for wildlife in the city.

With the blessing of the city arborist, Mark rehomes discarded plants from friends and council clean-ups to fill the naturestrip. His planting is eclectic and inclusive: conifers, tree ferns, cabbage trees, heliconias, liriopes and cycads grace the public space. Bird sown campanulata cherries and pseudopanax join the fray while roses salvaged from across the road are enjoying a jungle reprieve. "A lot of people around here don't have access to gardens.

This is here for them to enjoy. People with dogs and pushchairs stop and look, and children love it. It's my legacy," he says, adding: "If one human has managed to do this in 25 years, what are the other seven billion doing?"

Lush planting of subtropical plants and other people's discards has transformed a boring naturestrip into a luxuriant roadside garden for everyone to enjoy.

Taro and bromeliads cover the ground under a subtropical shrubbery at the end of the naturestrip.

Cherry blossom extending from Mark's garden mingles with the green canopy and subtropical palms of his roadside garden creating a bushy avenue.

Left:
Tillandsia and staghorn ferns adhere to the taller trees while fan palms and clivias grow amongst lush greenery below.

Lush greenery on edge of footpath.

Most people do stop and look at Mark's verdant verge which now extends to the corner of the street with a rapidly growing striking *Cycas taitungensis*.

Seed pods of a New Guinea impatiens.

Blue sky through a Cluster palm (*Chamaedorea costaricana*).

Striking silver foliage of a *Bromeliad puya venusta*.

Bromeliad aechmea species.

Old French street lamps and a row of pleached limes (Tilia cordata) planted hard against the wall create an uncanny sense of distance in a space that's actually no more than six or seven meters long.

CHAPTER 11

French Flair

I've always loved those little French courtyards. I peer in the gateways and sigh 'Oh yes!'

A tap trickles into a concrete trough; a rustic ladder leans against a wall overgrown with creepers; an old French grain sack makes do as a doormat.

Visitors may well feel they have stepped into a village in rural France, but the courtyard Barbara Bellis created is in the Antipodes is bounded by city streets on two sides and the back of the neighbor's garage on another.

The bijou garden, just half a dozen paces in any direction, belies its size. A pair of old French street lamps stand as a portal to a row of pleached limes planted hard against the front wall, creating an uncanny sense of distance.

The lightness of crusher dust underfoot adds to the illusion of expanse, while a large topiaried bird in a super-sized pot adds aerial scale.

It is the closest thing to a French cockerel in this garden, but a crowing rooster would not sound out of place in a courtyard that oozes Gallic charm. Over the years, Barbara has made regular pilgrimages to France, wandering around the villages, camera in hand, looking for inspiration for her garden back home. "I've always loved those little French courtyards. I peer in the gateways and sigh 'Oh yes!'"

A sense of effortless order is at the heart of French landscape design, along with a cool colour palette featuring whites, greens, blues and purples. In Barbara's version, clipped topiaries, buxus balls and spires of thuja add structure and a touch of formality amongst relaxed plantings of lavender, blue salvia and white geraniums, many of them in pots.

Simple rustic adornments like an old wooden wheelbarrow and galvanized watering can, seemingly casually placed, suggest it is siesta time in a working farmyard. The garden's serenity is further enhanced by invitations to rest throughout the garden: a pair of white wicker armchairs under an awning, a wooden seat between a pair of potted topiaries, a vintage deck chair.

At the end of the pleached lime "walkway" an outdoor table sits in the shade of a Nyssa sylvatica, a tree which delivers year-round with glossy green leaves in summer and scarlet foliage in autumn.

A trough and tap water feature between the trunks of pleached lindens has a shrine-like tranquility with its tall urns and potted miniature agapanthus.

Its fiery fall hues are matched by Boston ivy *(Parthenocissus tricusipata)* draped over the front entrance while the vigorous self-adhering climber Ficus pumila disguises the back of the neighbor's garage, suggesting it is a hedge not a plain block wall.

Gravel is another staple element of French gardens. The coarse limestone-rich crusher dust used in Barbara's garden. It exudes a gray-gold warmth, requires minimal maintenance and, best of all, she says Barbara: "You can walk on it in high heels."

IDEAS:

Pots add flexibility and formality to small courtyard garden, as well as charm. For the understated look that is at the heart of French chic, avoid gaudy or highly glazed surfaces.

Potted topiary spheres and white pelargoniums line the paved pathway to the house with ficus and a rustic ladder disguising the neighbor's garage wall.

A hand-hewn manuka ladder adds visual and vertical interest as well as providing a handy display rack for decorative items.

A tall candelabra adds a touch of classical elegance above a grouping of white petunias in terracotta pots.

An outdoor table, which doubles as a dining space and surface for more pots, sits in the shade of a *Nyssa silvatica* (Tupelo or Black Gum) tree.

Topiaries in classic urns and terracotta pots add structure and formality to the tranquil garden while lime-chip underfoot and ficus on the high walls softens the hard landscaping.

White wicker armchairs provide comfortable shaded seating on the north side of the house. Miniature bamboo, a popular plant in French courtyards, is planted in a galvanized urn on the far side.

A vintage deckchair under the lindens is one of several inviting resting spots.

Blue lavender and white pelargoniums make a classic French colour combination.

Potted topiary spheres and white pelargoniums line the paved pathway to the house with ficus and a rustic ladder disguising the neighbor's garage wall.

135

CHAPTER 12

In The Pink

An historic cottage complete with white picket fence is a charming picture in pink with roses tumbling through its small garden and spilling over the fence.

The full blooms of Rosa 'Albertine', a vigorous climber which is forgiven for its thorns by its form, colour and fragrance.

Flowers are food for the soul.

A picture in pink, draped with roses behind a white picket fence, this little colonial cottage is a much admired magnet for passers-by but could easily have been relegated to history's scrap heap.

The two bedroom workingman's cottage, built in the 1860s for a family of nine, was in a state of dilapidation when Sarah Smale bought it in 2001. She made it her mission to save the ailing abode, mending its bones and nursing it back to health.

Sarah saved the house but it was her successor, Jane Teasdale - an avid gardener with a penchant for pink - who dressed the elderly dwelling in a style befitting its years.

Originally one of a row of cottages, the sole survivor is squeezed onto a diminutive section. The front verandah is just a few paces from the street while the east side of the house has room for a little bricked patio, tiny lawn and pergola. Jane's solution to the space constraints: "I just filled it in with flowers".

Apart from a couple of camellias and a michelia out the back, the cottage garden is a profusion of roses, peonies, lilies, pelargoniums, sweet peas, aquilegias and lavender with self-seeding foxgloves and annuals filling any vacant spaces. "Flowers are food for the soul," says Jane, who has a particular passion for roses.

She has too many to name, and is not bothered by this. "I've never been interested in names and I don't keep plant tags. I either like it or I don't." Her most-favored is 'Mutabilis'. "I love it because it's like butterflies when it blooms and is always changing colour," says Jane, who also recommends carpet roses for their summer-long performance and easy-care disposition. "You just take to them with the hedge cutters."

Plants are chosen for their fragrance as well as their pinkness, and Jane has a pragmatic approach to gardening that allows her time to smell the roses. "I pack the garden with plants so I don't have to weed. I'm not an orderly gardener. I don't like things trimmed or planted in rows." She doesn't spray and happily lets plants seed themselves. "I think there's nothing prettier than a field of wildflowers."

A great believer in the power of flowers, Jane would pick posies for passers-by who stopped to admire the rose-strewn cottage. But, like Sarah, her work is done and the cottage has been passed into new hands for its next era.

It was an easy transition. "I walked in and fell in love," says Yvonne Thompson. In the capable hands of another gardener with a love of things past, the little cottage's future is looking rosy.

Roses in soft shades of pink blend with the walls of the former workingman's cottage, painted Resene Clam Shell (a pastel pearl pink beige) to harmonize with the rosy palette.

The violet hues of rambling Rosa 'Veilchenblau' join pink roses, lichnis and geraniums in the floriferous cottage garden.

IDEAS:

In praise of pink: Some people shy away from pink, but it is a colour that can enhance almost every garden. Mass-plantings in rosy hues will make a small space feel larger and brighter. Pink's palette can convey a range of moods from levity to romance. Hot-pink pops against a green background; pale pink creates an ethereal feel. Silver foliage is pink's perfect partner while blue blooms make compatible bed-fellows.

A white wicker chair enjoys a rosy view on the front verandah.

'The Fairy', a drought-tolerant and disease-resistant pale pink rose that flowers throughout summer, joins hot-pink pelargoniums below *Rosa* 'Veilchenblau'.

A standard 'Burgundy Iceberg' rose adds eye-level blooms along the side path.

Huge fragrant clusters of 'Wedding Day' rose hang over the path to a little bricked patio and lawn at the side of the cottage.

Below:
'Wedding Day' rose merges with a soft pink foxglove.

'Abraham Darby' rose, a fragrant David Austin cultivar, brings its rich apricot hues to the garden.

A black trellis provides support and a dark foil for the cascading bank of roses.

'Mutabilis' rose petals.

'Burgundy Iceberg' in full bloom.

The back of the two-bedroom house is smothered with roses and cottage perennials.

The front courtyard is both an outdoor gallery and place for quiet reflection with the central sculpture on a bed of dianella, and blue totara lining the walls.

CHAPTER 13

Garden Gallery

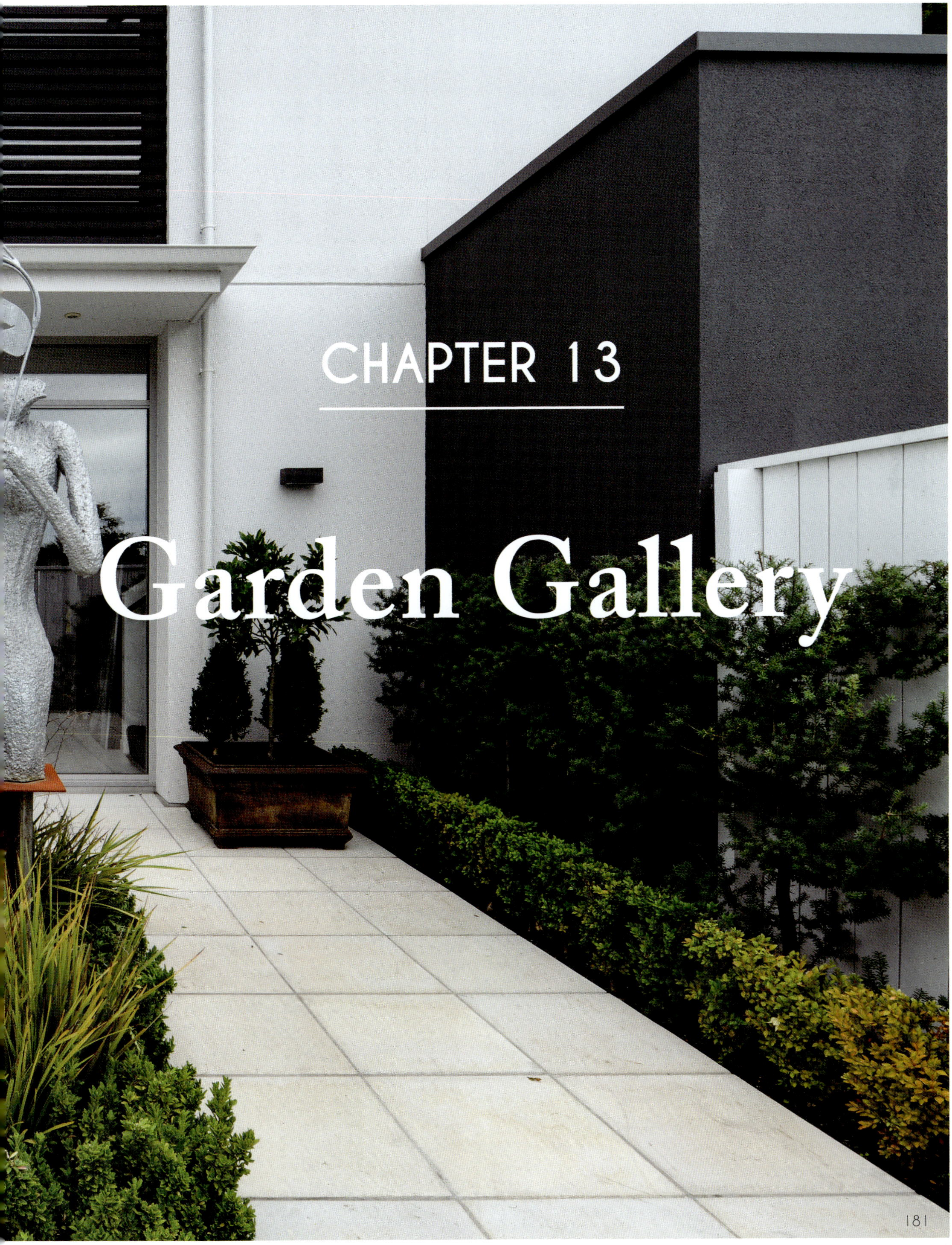

I'm always on the look-out for art. It makes a garden interesting.

A masked Venetian figure in the entrance courtyard is a larger-than-life clue that art and entertainment might play a central role in this household; a short walk through the house and out the other side confirms it.

The living area of Sandy and Clive Low's art-filled home flows onto an expansive deck which overlooks a garden designed for both convivial living and showcasing their sculptures.

Seemingly mid-bounce above the stream, a large blue ball holds center stage. *The Sky Has Fallen,* by Rebecca Rose, is constructed out of metal shields but appears weightless mounted on its concealed stand. Nearby, a work by sculptor Allan O'Loughlin depicts a woman swinging a small child in her arms. "I'm always on the look-out for art. It makes a garden interesting," says Sandy.

The symmetry extends onto the street with pittosporums, red flax and low buxus flanking a paved pathway that wraps around the central sculpture before continuing to the front door.

A metal café table is both decorative and functional in the high-walled outdoor room.

Left:
Allan O'Loughlin's masked figure holds center stage while Unfolding, a hand hammered stainless steel flower by Ken Laws, adorns the gray wall.

IDEAS:

Large sculptures make striking statements as well as being visually interesting conversation pieces. Over-sized objects make small areas look bigger, giving character and scale as well as a strong focal point. As with interiors, a small room furnished only with little things risks resembling an unstructured doll's house.

Apart from the aesthetic attraction, large focal points add another dimension to small spaces. "Over-scaled pieces give the feeling that the area is a lot bigger than it is, which is the opposite effect to what you would expect," says landscape architect Ben McMaster who designed the garden for the couple and their two sons.

Family, friends, food and fine art are the cornerstones on which the Lows have created their suburban sanctuary and, as well as providing a gallery for their artworks, the compact backyard has 'rooms' set aside for playing, eating and entertaining.

It wasn't an easy brief, as the site drops steeply to a creek on the lower boundary which meant any hardscaping and planting on the bank was limited by the city council's riparian requirements.

Ben's solution was to float a cantilevered deck over the slope. Running the breadth of the house, it flows seamlessly from the interior and, with built-in seating and a gas fire place, has a lounge-like feel. Large umbrellas on swivels at each corner can be positioned for all weather conditions. "We live on the deck," says Sandy of the alfresco dining and entertaining area which has a swimming pool set in at the far end.

Below, a boardwalk steps down to the stream with two tiny lawns either side. Blue totara, griselinia and miniature toetoe form the living walls of the outdoor rooms while the floors are carpeted with grasses, red flaxes and variegated dianella.

Ben chose plants for their form and texture to complement the man-made sculptures. Irregular spheres of wiry muehlenbeckia, silver spears of astelia and canopies of golden kowhai add their own artistry to the garden.

Set close to the house wall, the small swimming pool is screened from the main deck area by a blue totara hedge and layered lush garden that is also home to a life-size figurative sculpture. The pool cover rolls away under the decking at left to maximise space in the small area.

Dark pewter walls are an effective backdrop for both the metal artwork and foliage below.

Mother and Child by sculptor Allan O'Loughlin.

The Sky Has Fallen, by Rebecca Rose, appears to hover over the creek at the bottom of the garden, with the round forms and waving heads of miniature toetoe adding to the sense of lightness.

Wooden steps lead from the upper deck to the creek, bisecting the two small lawns.

Rebecca Rose's sculptural ball, constructed out of small metal shields, adds texture as well as vibrant colour to the garden.

Muehlenbeckia and griselinia border the small lawn below the pool, suggesting greater length and drawing the eye to the blue ball.

A line-up of colorful cushions sets a convivial mood on the deck, with blankets and the gas fire at the ready should the temperature drop and cantilevered umbrellas furled and waiting for the sun. The dense lush backdrop, which abounds with birdlife, adds to the sense of enclosure.

The diminutive courtyard, viewed over pots of white pelargoniums on the upstairs balcony, is a thoughtfully ordered outdoor room.

CHAPTER 14

The Front Room

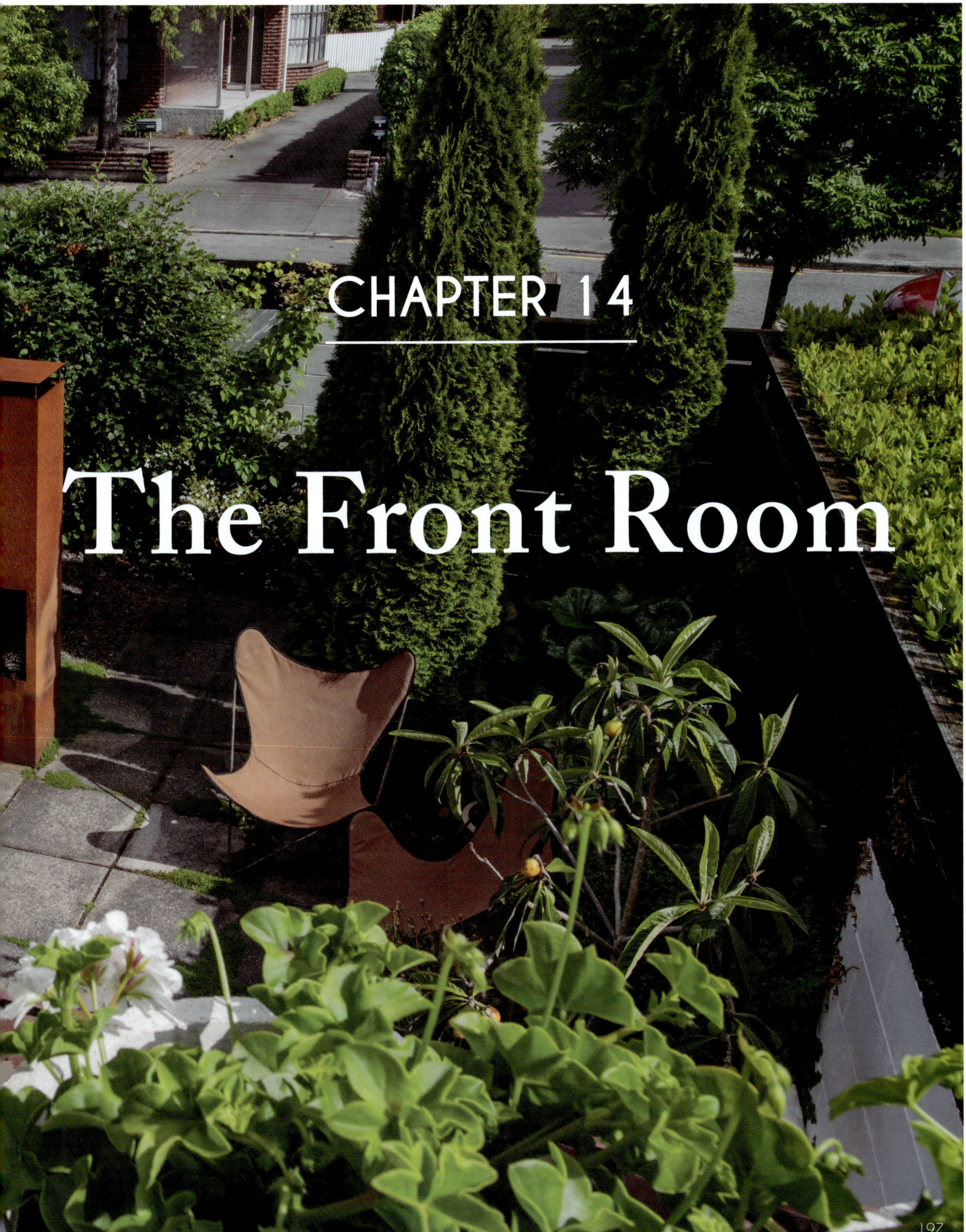

Potted marsh grasses add lightweight height and texture at eye-level as well as movement.

I use every bit of my house and garden. My courtyard is simply another room.

Juliet Mannering's townhouse garden is an extension of her home, both physically and conceptually. Both are understated yet evocative and true to her maxim that less is more.

The 1970s concrete block and timber abode is the work of Sir Miles Warren, an architect known for his distinctive modernist style. "There's a simplicity and honesty to his buildings," says Juliet, who has adopted the same pared back principles in the courtyard garden.

The garden, a mere 45 m^2, sits between the house and street with high walls and fences on three sides and opening from the living room through nearly wall-width sliding doors on the fourth. The white concrete block walls of the house continue through to the garden, unifying the two zones. With the footprint of the house not much bigger than that of the garden, the contents of both small spaces are carefully considered. "I use every bit of my house and garden," says Juliet. "My courtyard is simply another room."

Like the house, the outdoor room is classic Warren in black, brown and white. Its focal point, visually and socially, is a corten steel cooking fire and large square table. Deep cedar slatted seats, which double as daybeds (and occasionally night-time ones too), are covered with brown fabric, as are the sun umbrella and pair of canvas butterfly chairs.

Black and white awnings and striped cushions add to the monochromatic simplicity of the enclosure which is bordered with high dark-stained horizontal paling fences and white block walls. The side fences are softened with ficus while hydrangea petiolaris clings to the front wall and the square pavers are outlined with a trim of creeping ground thyme.

Juliet sculpts rather than paints with her plants, selecting them for their form and texture rather than colour. A diminutive grove of pleached English beech trees planted on a patch of river stones creates vistas through, under and over as well as inviting exploration of the narrow path behind. Across the way, a trio of towering Thuja occidentalis 'Smaragd' seem to be in conversation inside the gate, while three trimmed pots of muehlenbeckia form giant inverted lampshades, repeating the form of hanging cane lightshades inside the house. Long-stemmed marsh grasses sway in tall pots, their rusty seed heads repeating the colour of the corten steel.

She favors shades of brown and green. "I like neutral colors because they are peaceful to live around and you don't tire of them." A bank of inky blue-black and rusty irises, planted in memory of a pet dog of the same name, throw a rare dark splash of seasonal colour. "Most of my plants are there for personal reasons, either as a memory of people close to me or gifted by good friends," says Juliet of her garden that only has room for the things she loves.

Attention to form, colour and detail in this small space is seen in a neat arrangement of pinecones in the fire and angle-cut muehlenbeckia peeking from behind.

Left:
The rusty seed heads of the grasses pick up the colour of the corten steel.

IDEAS:

Consider qualities other than colour and texture when choosing plants. Swaying grasses give movement to a static space while other plants perform even in inclement conditions. Raindrops cling to the bare twisted twigs of muehlenbeckia in winter, while droplets sit like tiny ball-bearings on the felted gray-green leaves of *Alchemilla mollis* (Lady's Mantle).

Verticality is important on a small footprint, demonstrated here with lofty thujas, tall grasses in pots and the chimney-like outdoor oven stretching above the high fences.

Brown canvas butterfly chairs add another simple form to the carefully edited landscape while respecting the colour scheme. A long-fingered loquat and large-leafed ligularia both contrast and balance the tall tight forms of a corner grouping of *Thuja occidentalis* 'Smaragd'.

The loquat provides dappled shade over the corner seat which is partially screened by a large Marlborough rock daisy in an old copper pot with little cypress balls and variegated iris in pots at its feet. Juliet uses the terracotta tiles stacked on table as outdoor coasters.

A lemon tree grows behind a border of rosemary, while star jasmine (*Trachelospermum jasminoides*) grows on the block house wall and ficus on the fence. Black-and-white cushions on the brown-squabbed seats reinforce the simple colour palette.

Lighting amplifies the positive and negative spaces at night, with angle-cut muehlenbeckia in pots dramatically framing a slender beech trunk with the glow bringing out the texture of the gravel and climbing hydrangea foliage on the wall behind.

Left:
English beech trees add their layer above the trimmed triangular meuhlenbeckia. "I call them my 'Trumpets' because they look like the ice-creams," says Juliet, who opted for continuing the line of the pots rather than clipping them into balls. "They look beautiful in winter when drops of rain cling to their bare branches."

Far Left:
Hydrangea petiolaris grows over the wall behind a pair of old concrete urns by the front gate.

Above: Star jasmine (*Trachelospermum jasminoides*).

Below: Marlborough rock daisy (*Pachystegia rufa*).

English beech trees grow in patch of gravel while hydrangea petiolaris clambers up the front wall, adding an element of wilderness to the tiny courtyard.

A trompe l'oeil Tuscan landscape overhung with orange 'Westerland' rose and flanked by twisty topiaries is just one of the illusory tricks used in a garden designed to bring pleasure to both its occupants and visitors.

CHAPTER 15

Garden of Illusion

There's nothing wrong with a bit of fake.

Visitors might rest under a pillared colonnade or linger at the 'Trevi Fountain' before heading for a stroll down a poplar-lined avenue. Yet this Italian idyll is not what it seems. It is a small Antipodean garden designed by Mo Sutton, mistress of illusion.

Using trompe l'oeil deceptions, strategically placed mirrors and clever landscaping, she has created a colorful retreat with Tuscan overtones on a 496 m^2 corner section.

When Mo and her husband, Graham, built on the bare section in 2005, they extended the house close to the boundaries with verandahs, leaving space for a slim moat of vegetation between their home and high concrete block walls shielding them from the street. Mo then set about maximizing the effect of the garden strips, some of which were barely a meter wide. "The challenge is to go up instead of out or it would feel very narrow," she says.

She started by establishing ficus on the plastered block walls, turning them into high green hedges, and planting clematis up the house to draw the eye further skywards. Within the garden beds towering cypress, clipped yews and small weeping trees now oversee borders

Ficus clings to a pillar under the north-facing colonnade while roses of every hue join delphiniums behind a low buxus hedge in the narrow front garden.

A bust and birdbath on plinths are focal points through the rose-draped archway at the end of the vegetable garden.

IDEAS:

High walls help trap fragrance in a confined space. This can be accentuated by covering them with scented climbers and planting a potpourri of perfumed flowers and herbs in the beds below.

packed with texture and colour and underplanted with more demure heuchera, mondo grass and ferns.

Despite its scale, the garden has all the elements of a natural forest with its canopy, middle plantings and undergrowth. "The greenness and structure are always there. I can make it look sharp or let it grow wild, and it's still lovely with its bare bones in winter."

In summer, the small garden is a riot of colour from roses in vibrant shades of orange to pink dahlias ("you've got to have a bit of hot pink") and sweet peas scrambling through the perennials.

"When the roses are out the scent is absolutely heady," she says. The fragrance is intensified by the garden's containment, particularly in the vegetable garden along the back where a narrow pathway means brushing past lavender, rosemary and thyme.

With every centimeter planted, the garden is kept healthy with regular doses of liquid fertilizer, although not everything always required feeding.

While waiting for her slow-growing evergreen clematis to become established, Mo augmented it with artificial ivy for instant greenery and popped in a couple of fake hostas as temporary fillers.

"There's nothing wrong with a bit of fake. It's just about getting that balance right," says Mo, who has placed mirrors throughout the garden, magnifying and lightening small spaces as well as suggesting possibilities beyond.

And there is more: With council permission, Mo has extended the garden beyond its high walls and planted a garden on the naturestrip to enrich the streetscape. A trio of Indian bean trees grow over beds of hydrangeas, astilbes and liriopes while roses escape the interior to spill over the top of the wall and charm passers-by.

The full-blown blooms of 'Westerland' rose are a soft contrast to the more formal structure of pencil cypresses and the high ficus-clad wall behind.

Bright green planters along the strip on the east side of the house are packed with herbs and vegetables.

A circular mirror gives David a beatific air.

'Rhapsody in Blue'.

The pillared verandah on the northwest side has glazed skylights to further enhance the indoor-outdoor feel. The striped flowers of 'Claude Monet' rose are in the foreground.

'Alexander of Kent'.

'Mother's Day'.

The garden's classical theme continues with Adrienne pouring water in a mirrored grotto.

The soft salmon blooms of 'Phyllis Bide' rose hang over a walkway through pencil cypresses to an urn and mirror at the far end. The tall conifers alongside the narrow path exaggerating the sense of distance.

'Phyllis Bide' spills over the top of the garden wall where Mo has planted the naturestrip for the pleasure of passers-by under the shade of Indian bean trees. Richly colored planting behind a lush border of liriopes includes 'Sally Holmes' and 'Mutabilis' roses, hydrangeas and astilbes. The ficus on the wall is kept tidy with a hedge trimmer and Mo keeps the base clear to ensure it doesn't sucker through the garden.

'Sally Holmes' rose scales the wall from the roadside while 'Westerland' peeks over the top.

'Mutabilis'.

Steel obelisks add verticality as well as cages to contain the roses and prevent their thorny limbs from grabbing passers-by.

Mo's garden is higher than it is wide with arches, tall cypresses and climbing plants creating an overhead tapestry that is full of scent as well as colour.

'Westerland'.

Behind the high walls of the secluded outdoor seating area is the busy street corner. Pots, pillars, bamboo trellising and topiaries give structure to the layered enclave.

Strong hardscaping defines a courtyard with a focus on honest materials and informal planting.

CHAPTER 16

Natural Connections

The terrace looks over the courtyard to kowhai and pohutukawa trees which give privacy without blocking the view at the far end. The lower lounge sits alongside the lawn at left.

I wanted it to feel as though nature was reclaiming the land.

Kris and Jess Sowersby's hillside home is reminiscent of a Russian stacking doll: the house is nestled into the landscape and the garden is nestled into the house.

A courtyard garden had been at the top of the couple's wish list. "You see a lot of outdoor spaces not being used because they are too exposed to the elements. We thought if we encapsulated it within our house we would use it more," says Jess.

The arms of their U-shaped house embrace a courtyard which is bordered on the fourth side by a fence. By pushing the building towards the boundaries of the 490 m^2 site, they allowed the dwelling to enfold the most usable outdoor space rather than leaving it as a skin around the edges.

Both the house and courtyard are on two levels, following the contour of the gently sloping site.

Where the wings step down to the master bedroom on one side and lounge on the other, the courtyard drops from an upper paved terrace to a lower flat lawn. "It has the feel of a conversation pit which fits with our love of 1970s architecture," says Jess.

Extensive glazing keeps a constant connection between the house and garden, the latter also providing a secure play area for the couple's young daughter and dog. At its heart, a slatted cedar and steel pergola adds a sculptural as well as practical element to the sometimes too-sunny sanctum.

Their brief to landscape architect Mark Newdick was simple: They wanted a "semi-unkempt Japanese-inspired garden" with a naturalistic feel. Their preference was for a muted palette, favoring greenery over flowers and with a focus on textured plants and "honest" surfaces that matched the simplicity of the house: timber, concrete, gravel, paving stones, rocks. "We wanted it to feel organic rather than manicured," says Kris. "We like overgrown," adds Jess.

Mark first went around the neighborhood to get a feel for the area and its vegetation, then set about establishing a garden that would look as if it had always been there. "Gardens are a small expression of the bigger ecological picture," he says. "I wanted to make it feel as though nature was reclaiming the land."

Trees have been positioned to screen out the house next door without compromising the views while relaxed plantings below feature robust textured plants. Silvery sword-like leaves of astelia sit alongside wiry muehlenbeckia and coprosma with flaxes and grasses, particularly dynamic in windwept locations, clumped amongst them. Pohutukawa and kowhai, with seasonal floral shows of red and yellow, add their star qualities to what is less a garden than a carefully curated natural habitat.

Rectangular forms anchor the garde from the tall windows of the house to the inset concrete pavers and terrac wall and steps. A tall olive tree, whic can be uplit at night, adds further verticality and softens the roofline.

The floor-to-ceiling window of the master bedroom, seen here with the pergola reflected, reinforces the vertical stained cedar cladding as well as offering grand views of the garden.

Thyme and marjoram grow amongst grasses and flaxes, adding fragrance and pleasing the bees.

IDEAS:

The internal courtyard has many virtues, especially where wind and changeable temperatures are the norm. Courtyards provide year-round shelter for both plants and people, as well as an intimate connection between house and garden. Private, child-safe and secure, they are the apogee of indoor-outdoor flow.

Left:
The pergola's steel struts add to the strong structural elements in a courtyard.

Below:
Concrete, cedar and steel are juxtaposed to convey a simplicity that is complimented by naturalistic planting.

The slatted cedar pergola joins the olive tree in shading the sunny terrace which is paved with free-form of schist stonework.

Vertical impressions from the timber boxing add rawness to the terrace wall, on which the attached pergola struts have been tapered to add to its sense of weightlessness and keep out of the way of the lawn mower.

Succulents and cacti thrive on the hot sheltered terrace.

Corokia, muehlenbeckia, karo, pimelia and lancewoods line the pathway down the side of the house with the gold of Gossamer grass *(Anemanthele)* growing through the silvery foliage of *Brachyglottis* 'Otari Cloud' in the foreground.

Coriander is amongst a prolific array of herbs and vegetables growing in raised planter boxes on the north side of the house.

The muted tones of kowhai, corokia, poa cita, lancewood and sand daphne *(Pimelia prostrata)* compliment the utilitarian fibre-cement cladding and corten steel numbers, linking house and garden and creating a sense of calm

Wrought iron espalier frames give structure to a courtyard garden filled with edibles and flowering perennials.

CHAPTER 17

Framed with Fruit

We wanted less work and more food.

Fed up with their humdrum backyard, a resourceful couple is relishing its transformation into a productive plot that is as eye-catching as it is mouth-watering.

"Edible plants give you a wonderful seasonal garden and are a great way of using space," says landscape architect Robert Watson, who helped redesign Ross Palmer and Craig Seagar's townhouse garden.

When they purchased the property, the 8 m x 14 m x 8 m triangular garden, which opens from the house along the hypotenuse, comprised a tiny lawn with meter-deep borders along the fences.

When faced with a small space, the natural response is to push everything to the boundaries. In fact, one should do the opposite says Robert, whose design features high steel espalier frames for fruit trees set in a meter from the fences. This not only gives the garden vertical scale but also creates the illusion of space by suggesting there is more 'behind the hedge'.

The frames have been spray-painted black and timber trellises and fences stained dark charcoal, making them recede into the background while at the same time providing a sharp backdrop for foliage and flowers.

The rill runs from the far corner of the triangular garden.

IDEAS:

Espaliered fruit trees serve as useful structural elements as well as being productive, giving the effect of hedges without the on-going maintenance. The bare branches and steel arms make a striking feature in winter while also letting sunlight into the garden. In spring there is blossom and in summer shady foliage and glowing globes of ripe fruit.

The pond and courtyard can be seen through daubings of pink blossom on the espaliered 'Goldmine' nectarine and 'Gordons Glory' peach.

The bare branches of the nectarine make a striking skeleton in winter.

The out-stretched arms of the espaliered plum are clad in white blossom in spring.

A rill flowing from an obscured font in the far corner to a central pond further draws attention away from the boundaries. The lawn has gone and the courtyard laid with easy-care lime chip.

"We wanted less work and more food," says Craig, and their garden is scoring high on both counts. The espaliered nectarine, plum and peach are laden and a pair of quinces so bountiful that they must be quick to pick the fruit before the branches break. Berry bushes share their beds with leafy vegetables while herbs and seasonal dwarf beans flourish in pots.

"Nothing beats the simple pleasure of walking out and picking your own produce," says Craig. And they are happy to share it with friends, both human and winged, the fruit trees and berries attracting birds to the garden as well as providing blooms for bees. The edibles are interspersed with flowering perennials and anchored with groundcovers, a gentle undercurrent of blue linking the garden elements. Small clouds of catmint and scrambling 'Rozanne' geranium grow under fruit trees while the powdery leaves of *Hosta* 'Big Daddy' lighten a dark corner.

The pond is edged with bluestone paving and filled with luminous water irises while, alongside, a steel-blue table and pair of chairs make an inviting place for contemplation as well as dining. With the sound of trickling water, delicate fragrance of blossom and taste of handpicked fruit, this is a garden for all the senses as well as all the seasons.

A narrow rill runs from a hidden corner font to a central pond bordered with bluestone paving and planted with water irises. The charcoal painted trellis, chosen to add vertical texture on one boundary, is seen through the espalier frame, while a vigorous Virginia creeper covers the neighbor's concrete block garage wall at right.

Come late summer, the plum is laden with fruit.

In winter, the leafless espalier frames and high trellis on the back fence add a strong geometric element to the garden.

By late spring, greenery is softening the vertical structures and forget-me-nots blurring the hard edges of the pathway pavers.

Set in from the boundaries, the espaliers frame views of the garden from both sides. Blue flowers abound in the garden from ajuga spires and forget-me-nots to *Nepeta* 'Six Hills Giant' and the ebullient *Geranium* 'Rozanne'.

A scented garden outside the bedroom features herbs growing amongst lavender, cornflowers and a white 'Margaret Merrill' rose, while a vigorous cloak of Virginia creeper covers the neighbor's concrete block garage wall to the side.

In summer, the espaliered 'Goldmine' nectarine and 'Gordons Glory' peach make a leafy backdrop to the metal table and chairs.

Pink nectarine blossom.

White plum blossom.

Charcoal fencing makes a dark foil for the pink blossoms of the nectarine and peach

Bountiful crop of plums.

Fruiting peach.

The laden plum and stems of *Nepeta* 'Six Hills Giant' catmint partially screen the bronze torso by Terry Stringer and corner font.

Left:
Relaxed plantings of perennials under the fruiting plum include common poppies *(Papaver rhoeas)*, white peonies, *Astilbe* 'Webi Gloria', *Nepeta* 'Six Hills Giant' and the ebullient blue *Geranium* 'Rozanne' (far right) which flowers well into autumn.

Above:
The large blue-gray leaves of *Hosta* 'Big Daddy' lighten the shady far corner while a solitary quince hangs over the bronze sculpture.

Bluestone pavers laid in lime-chip.

Set a meter out from the fences, the espalier frames partition the central courtyard from the paths alongside.

Layering and the controlled interplay of green, white and black has turned a boxed-in section into a peaceful enclave.

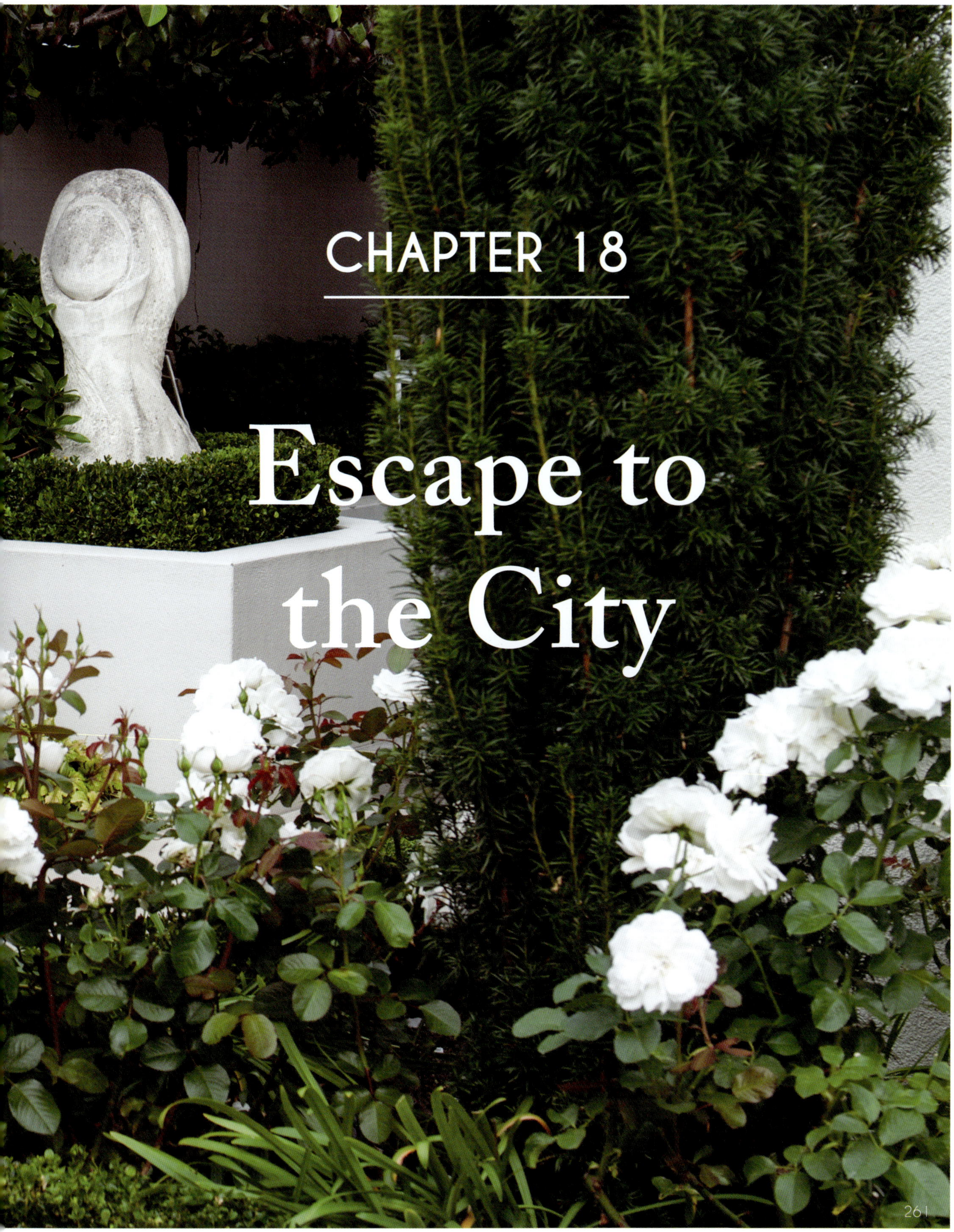

CHAPTER 18

Escape to the City

When you've got a small space, you've got to get it right because it's always on view.

When Chris and Jude Trengrove moved to town, they traded green pastures and a park-like garden for a small city section boxed in by houses on all sides. Yet through the layered planting of evergreens, they have created an equally verdant if less expansive outlook.

"When you've got a big country garden, you can have a bit going on here and a bit going on there. When you've got a small space, you have to make choices and you have to get it right because it's always on view," says Jude, who

Evergreen oaks *(Quercus ilex)* controlled as standards provide a structured canopy in the north-facing courtyard where black and white table settings are separated by an eye-catching limestone sculpture. The rooms are further defined by a subtle change in level from raised timber decking to concrete pavers.

opted for the simplicity of green and white for a garden that would look good year-round with minimal maintenance.

The narrow garden, which wraps around three sides of the house, has been cleverly re-structured to give the impression of depth and height. Hedges grow above hedges which grow above low walls. Tall evergreen oaks and yews tower over leafy shrubs which drop to borders of black and green mondo and crisply clipped buxus.

The Trengroves, started by topping the wooden fence with a trellis for additional privacy, painting it black and espaliering star jasmine along its length. Existing sasanqua camellias, previously dotted through the garden, were regrouped to form hedges below.

When moving into an existing garden, a lot of decisions revolve around what should stay and what should go. A deciduous maple, crabapple and ornamental pear were spared for their year round performance in an otherwise-evergreen array. The pear *(Pyrus calleryana)* in particular, brilliantly represents all four seasons in a garden that doesn't change much from month to month. It has pure white flowers in spring, fresh green leaves in summer, blazes scarlet in autumn and makes a striking skeleton in winter.

Right:
Walls and monochromatic furnishings have been strategically placed to divide the small area into even smaller rooms, with layered greenery softening the hardscaping and a row of holm oaks *(Quercus ilex)*, tall English yew and evergreen magnolia providing shelter and a living screen from the Neighboring properties.

Right: One of a pair of Philippe Stark Bubble Club armchairs sits in the courtyard with a bed of 'Princess of Wales' white roses in the foreground and a raised bed featuring topiaries under a deciduous maple and trellis-topped wall behind.

Apart from this deciduous trio dropping a few bucketloads of leaves in autumn, there isn't much maintenance in this no-mess garden. "We can go quite a few weeks without doing anything," says Jude. The main job is clipping and, with mondo the only grass on the property, Chris has swapped his ride-on mower for a pair of hand shears and taken responsibility for trimming the hedges and topiaries.

The sharp, clean green of the garden is offset by monochromatic accessories, from white resin armchairs to a black birdbath. Hedges, low walls and furniture have been strategically placed to create rooms within the garden, with three distinct seating areas designed to catch the morning, afternoon and evening sun. Once too busy mowing lawns and pruning roses to often sit, the couple is enjoying this garden without being slaves to it.

An assortment of forms and foliage add interest to the garden, from clipped buxus balls, hedges and ducks to the glossy leaves of *Michelia doltsopa* 'Bubbles', a hybrid which has white scented flowers in spring. *Buxus sempervirens* 'Suffruticosa' was chosen over common box for its density and slower growth.

IDEAS:

Rather than having a separate vegetable patch that looks bleak off-season and takes up space in a small garden, leafy greens and seasonal edibles can be interspersed amongst the evergreen plants.

A limestone sculpture, seen here under the pear *(Pyrus calleryana)* in the early throes of its autumn colour change, adds a bold but organic presence to the garden.

Left:
The black table setting is echoed in the high dark trellising atop the wall.

Below: 'Princess of Wales', with its pure white flowers and healthy foliage, is the only rose in the garden.

The interplay of shape and texture, space and light transforms the small courtyard into an area that manages to be tranquil yet dynamic.

Right: Angled timber decking visually extends the narrow strip between the house and high wall on the east side, where the breakfast area opens to the kitchen.

A layered garden rises from its home ground to the top of a boundary fence and beyond, making the most of mature trees in the park next door.

CHAPTER 19

Parkside in the City

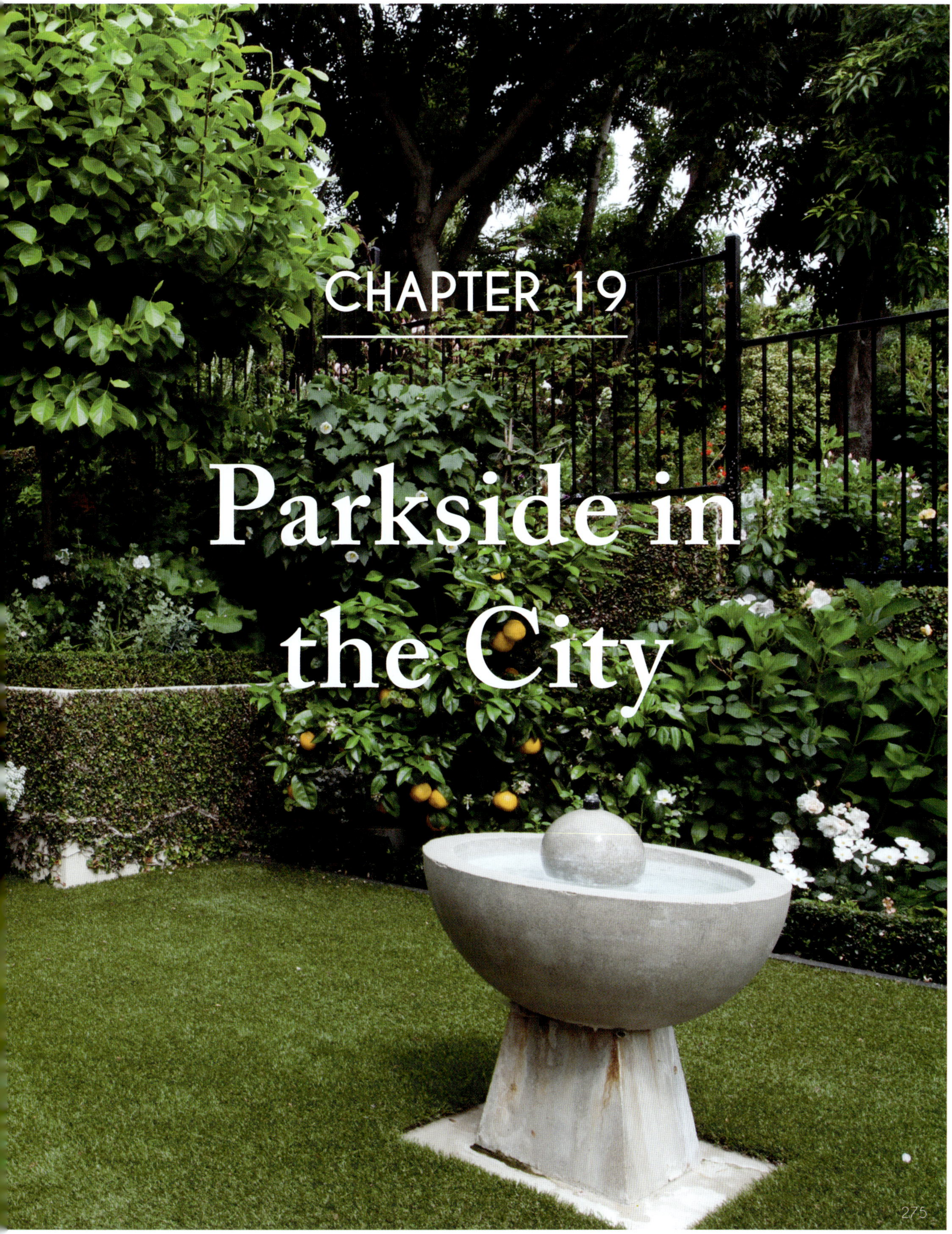

It gives me great pleasure watching children picking my flowers in the park.

When Kirsty Shiach and Ian Witters moved into an apartment alongside a park, it gave them the opportunity to reap the benefits of both worlds: an easy-care enclave with a backdrop of established trees.

The couple's courtyard garden draws the eye up from ground level through layered planting, over the top of a black steel fence to the green expanse and mature trees of the neighboring reserve.

After purchasing the apartment in 2010, the first thing they did was remove most of the existing tropical garden. "I wanted a more traditional garden with seasonal change," says Kirsty, who selected plants for their texture,

A neat skin of ficus, kept tightly clipped with hedge trimmers, covers the high curved wall creating a green backdrop for a pair of *Cercis canadensis* 'Forest Pansy' over arching the layered garden below. Inset paving under the table makes the artificial turf appear all the more natural.

The interplay of shape and texture, space and light transforms the small courtyard into an area that manages to be tranquil yet dynamic.

The rectangular garden feels at once contained yet open, nestled into the rising bank on the side boundary but with expansive park views to the north-east.

Contrasting foliages of taro and Strawberry Begonia *(Saxifraga stolonifera)* with its dainty white flowers.

contrast and fragrance as well as year round interest. Staghorn ferns and taro leaves make a bold backdrop for dainty white begonia, swaying spires of salvia, sweetly-scented jasmine and the soft blooms of old roses. Overhead, small deciduous trees like *Cercis canadensis* 'Forest Pansy', *Cercis* 'Texas White' and *Magnolia denudata* 'Alba' provide vertical structure and a filtered canopy.

Because of the garden's size, Kirsty opted for a restrained colour palette. "It would be hectic if it was too vibrant." The plant lover was less restrained with her planting, standardizing shrubs such as abutilon and fuchsia in order to pack more in but with an eye to keeping things orderly. "If a small garden is messy, it looks a shambles," she says.

The garden is anchored by a high curved wall covered with tightly-clipped ficus and a lower one topped with miniature Euonymus hedging. After a lawn of *Selliera microphylla* groundcover succumbed to the trampling of teenage feet, it was replaced with artificial grass made more realistic with set-in stepping stones.

Opening the apartment's large sliding doors creates a large indoor-outdoor entertaining area which is enhanced by uplights through the garden and a trickling water feature. "We used to have a big property with a tennis court and swimming pool, but this living space is almost more usable. We use every inch," says Kirsty.

With well-established planting and a computerized watering system, it takes just an hour or two a week to keep the garden in shape. "Downsizing has meant I spend time in the garden because I enjoy it rather than it being a chore."

A clipped buxus ball grows in a pot with a collar of white *Bacopa monnieri*, a perennial creeping herb.

The high metal fence provides separation without visually enclosing the garden. Mondo grass lines the risers of the steps to the park.

Below:
Texture and layering is seen at every level. Here, the citrus green bells of *Nicotiana langsdorffii* and soft blooms of white petunia sit over a neat hedge of miniature *Euonymus* on the top of the ficus-clad lower wall.

Over the fence

An avid gardener, Kirsty has borrowed more than the view from the park, planting a floral border on the other side of their shared boundary. "I started with a narrow strip of Heritage roses against the fence and it grew out from there," she says. The broad border is now packed with old roses including 'Stanwell Perpetual', 'Jean Ducher', 'Duchesse de Brabant', 'Lady Hillingdon' and *Rosa rugosa* 'Alba' as well as perennials and flowering annuals from cerinthe and pink mallow to sweet peas and angelica.

The bee-friendly garden includes borage and mignonette as well as salvias in half a dozen hues, seed heads for the birds and swan plants for the butterflies. And it's not just enjoyed by winged visitors. "It gives me great pleasure watching children picking flowers in the park," she says.

IDEAS:

Standardizing plants is a good way to create height and layering in a small garden without taking up too much space at ground level. Most bushy plants can be trained as standards, from fuchsias and heliotropes to rosemary and verbena. A row of standards can also be used to divide sections of the garden or add a touch of formality if tightly clipped.

Far Right:
The bed below the gate includes a blend of perennials and roses, including the delicate pink cinnamon-scented 'Stanwell Perpetual'.

The terrace offers more sheltered seating.

Far Left:
Kirsty's park-side garden started as a strip of roses but now is packed with perennials and flowering annuals that are encouraged to self-seed.

Left:
'Mutabilis' roses amongst bee-friendly plantings of mignonette, cerinthe and white borage.

Nicotiana langsdorffii.

Cape fuchsia *(Phygelius aequalis).*

'Stanwell Perpetual' rose.

'Lady Hillingdon' rose.

Meyer lemon.

Large English yew topiaries and sculptural plant forms feature in an inner-city courtyard garden bounded by buildings.

CHAPTER 20

Architect's Courtyard

I see it as the remains of an urban garden.

Gardens, like people, mature and grow old and if their bones are strong, the advancing years bring character rather than decay.

In the 1960s, Sir Miles Warren, internationally-reputed modernist architecture, designed an apartment that would double as his business premises. Integral to it, in an 8 m by 16 m void between buildings that had been a car yard, he made a garden.

"I've always been interested in gardens as part of the architectural process. I see it as a natural relationship," says Sir Miles.

His inner-city garden is a restful and orderly urban oasis, both inspired and defined by the limitations of space. "It's more about form than colour," he says. Both during inception and now its backbone is a central pool laid perpendicular to the apartment. A rill of irregular rectangles, it suggests symmetry without being static and divides the garden into two very different territories.

A narrow central pool divides the wild west from the tamer eastern territory. The mossy stone cap adds an historical architectural element.

Excavated soil from the pool was used to raise the garden on the west side, where less formal plantings grow behind blocks of limestone and a narrow path runs alongside the yew hedge boundary. The other side, edged with sharp granite and featuring a row of formal English yew topiaries, is more structured and echoes the architectural forms of the surrounding buildings.

The pool invites reflection in every sense of the word as well as attracting insects and birds, including ducks which come to nest and raise their families in spring. Some incarnations through the decades have seen waterlilies and irises growing amongst the sculptures.

Another era began when Sir Miles built a private art gallery on the east boundary, digging up the original lawn and hand-laying granite setts in a fan pattern.

With the passage of time, lanky saplings have filled out and grown tall, some succumbing to the chainsaw as they loomed too large. Their roots have pushed up the sett paving, adding meandering rifts to the design.

Nature, first coaxed by human hands, is marching to the beat of her own drum. The once tightly clipped yew pepper-pots are now a posse of winged Brobdingnagians towering over the pool. Supersized yuccas have been joined by a rogue cabbage tree behind the pond, where rocks have been added to keep the garden from spilling into the water. Acanthus and dianella are muscling out less forceful bed-mates.

"I see it as the remains of an urban garden," rues its now-nonagenarian creator. But it is much more than that. Blessed with good bones, the architect's garden is an abiding if wilder version of its younger self.

IDEAS:

Wabi-sabi, a Japanese concept with its roots in Zen, nurtures three simple realities: nothing lasts, nothing is finished, nothing is perfect. Wabi-sabi is about appreciating the beauty that comes with age and imperfection, an aesthetic pertinent in time-worn gardens.

The different textures and surface treatments either side of the rill add to the garden's strong form keeping the opposing forces at bay.

Euphorbia.

White camellia.

Clay "drainpipe people" in the pool, are dwarfed by the giant topiary guarding the east bank.

The view from the second floor of the apartment shows the enclosed nature of the courtyard garden, with the shuttered walls and slate roof of Sir Miles' art gallery at right.

Granite sett paving echoes the circular forms of the yew topiaries while an *Acer griseum* (Paperbark maple), with its distinctive peeling bark provides contrasting texture, form and colour.

Acanthus leaves.

Red camellia.

Dianella niagra berries.

Acer griseum bark.

Looking through foliage on the west side of the pond to the former apartment, now architectural offices, and single-story gallery. The fourth cube and ball yew topiary, at the far right, was planted in 1980.

ACKNOWLEDGEMENTS

Our thanks to the garden owners and designers who made this project possible by so generously sharing their inspiration, knowledge and beautiful small spaces.

First published in 2020 by New Holland Publishers
Sydney • Auckland

Level 1, 178 Fox Valley Road, Wahroonga, NSW 2076, Australia
5/39 Woodside Ave, Northcote, Auckland 0627, New Zealand

newhollandpublishers.com

A catalogue record for this book is available from the National Library of Australia.

ISBN 9781760792350

Group Managing Director: Fiona Schultz
Publisher: Sarah Beresford
Project Editor: Elise James
Designer: Yolanda La Gorcé
Cover Images: Barbara Bellis' French Courtyard, Anne Bassett's tranquil courtyard, Chris and Jude Trengrove's small city courtyard
Back Cover Image: Jeffares' rooftop garden
Production Director: Arlene Gippert

Printer: Toppan Leefung Printing Limited

10 9 8 7 6 5 4 3 2 1

Keep up with New Holland Publishers:
NewHollandPublishers
@newhollandpublishers